THE ILLUSTRATED NATURAL HISTORY

Scientific Consultants to the Series:

Lake Superior

OF CANADA The Great Lakes ROBERT THOMAS ALLEN

Earth Science Consultant WALTER TOVELL, Director, Royal Ontario Museum. *Life Science Consultant* J. MURRAY SPEIRS, Department of Zoology, University of Toronto

Library of Congress Catalog Card Number: 75-105928
ISBN O-9196-4401-5
Natural Science of Canada Limited
58 Northline Road, Toronto 16, Ontario, Canada

Publisher: Jack McClelland
Editor-in-Chief: Peter Crabtree
Senior Editor: Michael Worek
Art Director: Peter Moulding
Visual Editor: Bill Brooks

Editorial Consultant: Pierre Berton

THE GREAT LAKES

Editors: Gerd Grossman / Michael Worek
Art Directors: Bill Fox / Peter Moulding
Picture Editor: Bill Brooks
Artists: Vlasta van Kampen / Jerry Kozoriz /
John Yates / Gordon McLean

Scarborough Bluffs

Contents

Prologue

THE BIGGEST LAKES IN THE WORLD

Author Allen warms up on a winter field trip on Bruce Peninsula.

Biting deep into the midriff of North America, dividing Canada from the United States, the Great Lakes lie like inland seas halfway across the continent, from the St. Lawrence to within eighty miles of the Mississippi, through forest, farmland and prairie, from the Alleghenies to the rocky hills of the Canadian Shield. They lace together some of the world's biggest cities throughout eight states, and a 2,362-mile coastline of Ontario. They dominate the agriculture, settlement, and pattern of life of a region bigger than France. Their old beaches, bottoms, deltas and sandbars are major features of the land. The lakes are a controlling factor in wild life. Animals adapting to their meadows, dunes and ancient lake plains have evolved into separate subspecies.

The Great Lakes are by far the largest body of fresh water on earth. They cover an area bigger than New Brunswick, Nova Scotia, Prince Edward Island and Newfoundland combined. People in other parts of North America, where a lake is something you can row across with a picnic lunch, can hardly picture them. Although every schoolchild knows what they look like on a map, nobody ever sees them this way. They're much too big.

A satellite orbiting 600 miles above the earth can photograph the whole chain of lakes – Ontario, Erie, Huron, Superior and Michigan – but at this height they are so faint they have to be pencilled in on weather maps. Seen from a plane their shorelines form such long, hazy, confusing angles that they are hard to relate to the surrounding land. Migrating birds following the west shore of Lake Erie, as they fly north in the spring, are gradually led south by the curve of the shore at Point Pelee until they find themselves heading south again.

Yet, although they hold enough water to cover all the land in Canada twelve feet deep, there seems no reason for the Great Lakes to be there at all. They have no mountain headwaters. They are fed by no glaciers or ice caps. Some of their contributing streams, like the Don or the Etobicoke near Toronto, are so shallow that within a mile or so of their outlets, a boy with a bit of luck can cross them on the cobbles without getting his shoes wet.

Their divides are in many places no more than low hills. You can stand in a small park in Chicago and watch the fast, shallow waters of the Des Plaines River flow toward the Gulf of Mexico, while the water a few blocks away drains toward Lake Michigan and the Gulf of St. Lawrence (at least, this would happen if the cutting of canals through the Chicago area had not changed the natural drainage of the region so that the Great Lakes can now be artificially connected to the Mississippi). Yet these low, inconspicuous divides control a drainage area that extends from a latitude almost as far south as New York City to within a hundred miles of James Bay. It is a region so great that it includes two climate zones, three main types of forest, some of the most intensely cultivated, heavily populated and industrialized sections on the continent, and areas of wilderness that look much as they did before man arrived on earth.

THE GREAT LAKES: AN ALBUM OF MAPS

The full colour maps on the following pages of this album were especially commissioned for the series to illustrate the most important aspects of the natural history of the Great Lakes region.

The photograph on the next two pages shows the area as seen from a satellite high above the earth.

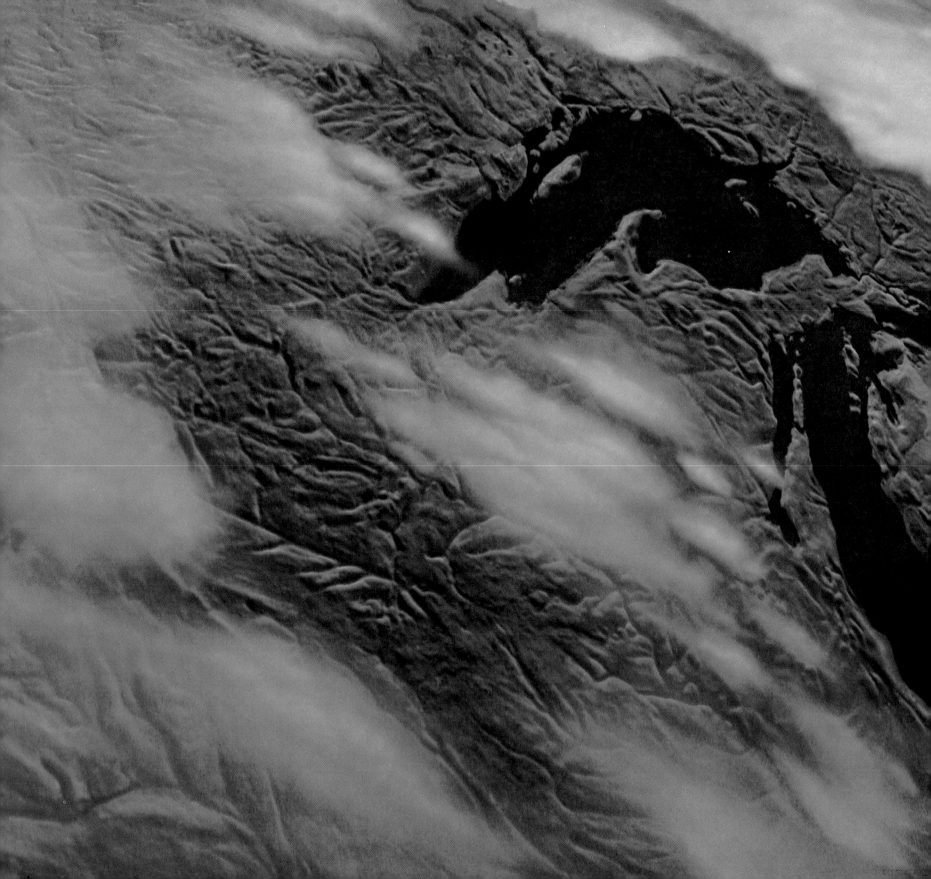

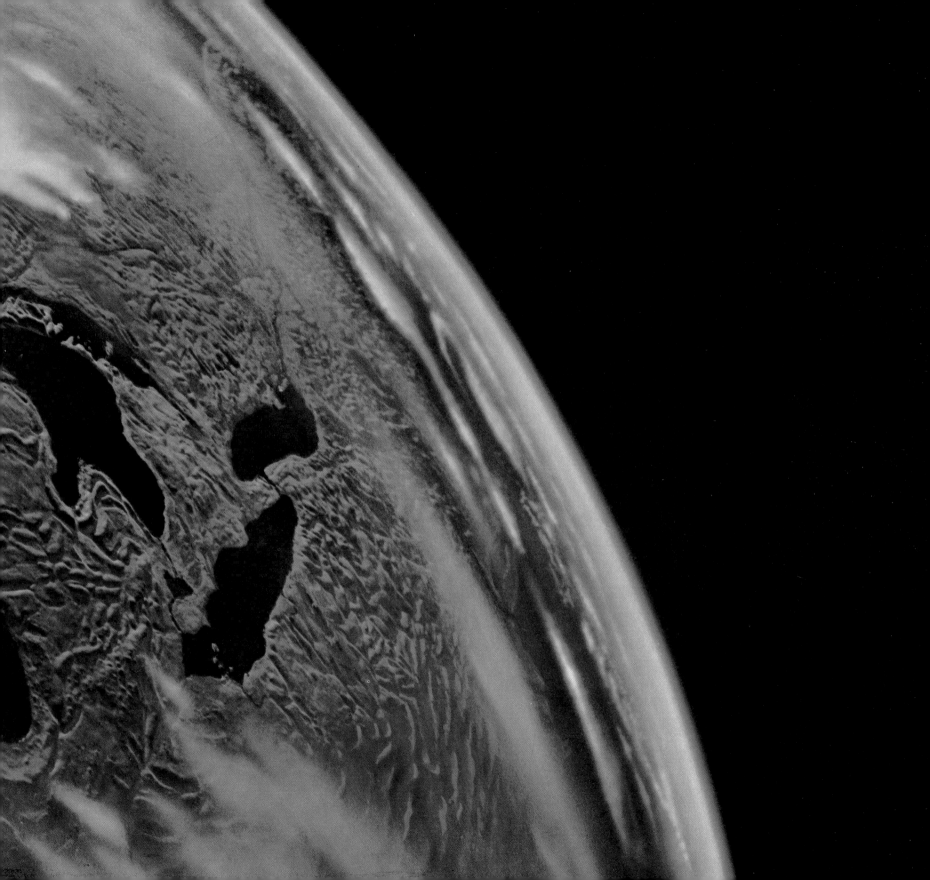

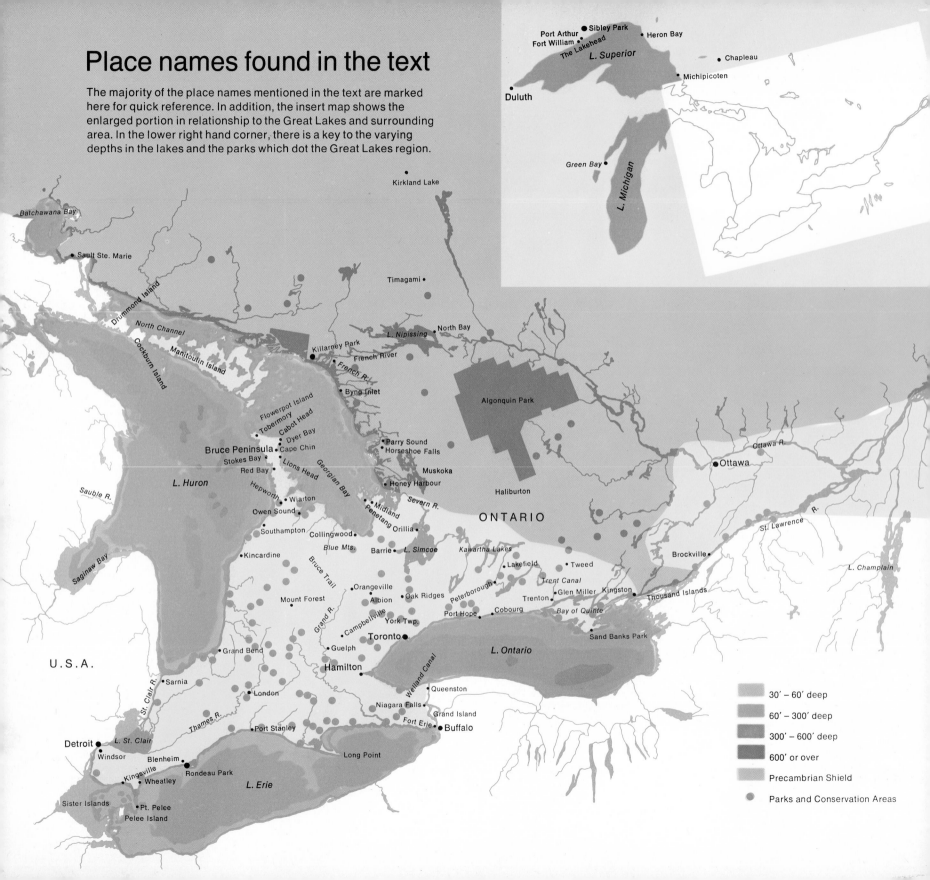

Place names found in the text

The majority of the place names mentioned in the text are marked here for quick reference. In addition, the insert map shows the enlarged portion in relationship to the Great Lakes and surrounding area. In the lower right hand corner, there is a key to the varying depths in the lakes and the parks which dot the Great Lakes region.

Port Arthur • Sibley Park
Fort William • • Heron Bay
The Lakehead
L. Superior • Chapleau
• Michipicoten
Duluth

Green Bay •
L. Michigan

Batchawana Bay

Kirkland Lake

• Sault Ste. Marie

Drummond Island
North Channel
Cockburn Island
Manitoulin Island

Timagami

L. Nipissing • North Bay
Killarney Park • French River
French R.
Byng Inlet

Algonquin Park

Flowerpot Island
Tobermory
Cabot Head
Dyer Bay
Bruce Peninsula • Cape Chin
Stokes Bay • Lions Head
Red Bay

Parry Sound
Horseshoe Falls

Muskoka

Ottawa R.

• Ottawa

L. Huron

Hepworth • Wiarton
Owen Sound

Georgian Bay

Honey Harbour
Midland
Penetang
Orillia

Severn R.

Haliburton

ONTARIO

St. Lawrence R.

Sauble R.

Southampton
Collingwood
Blue Mts.
Kincardine

Bruce Trail

Barrie • L. Simcoe

Kawartha Lakes

Lakefield • Tweed

Brockville

L. Champlain

Saginaw Bay

Mount Forest

Orangeville
Albion • Oak Ridges
Grand R.

Peterborough

Trent Canal
Trenton
Glen Miller Kingston
Thousand Islands

Campbellville
York Twp.
Grand Bend • Guelph
Toronto

Port Hope
Cobourg
Bay of Quinte

Sand Banks Park

U.S.A.

Hamilton

L. Ontario

Sarnia
London

Welland Canal
Queenston
Niagara Falls
Grand Island
Fort Erie • Buffalo

Thames R.
Port Stanley

Long Point

Detroit
L. St. Clair
Windsor
Blenheim
Kingsville • Rondeau Park
Wheatley
Sister Islands
Pt. Pelee
Pelee Island

L. Erie

30' – 60' deep
60' – 300' deep
300' – 600' deep
600' or over
Precambrian Shield
● Parks and Conservation Areas

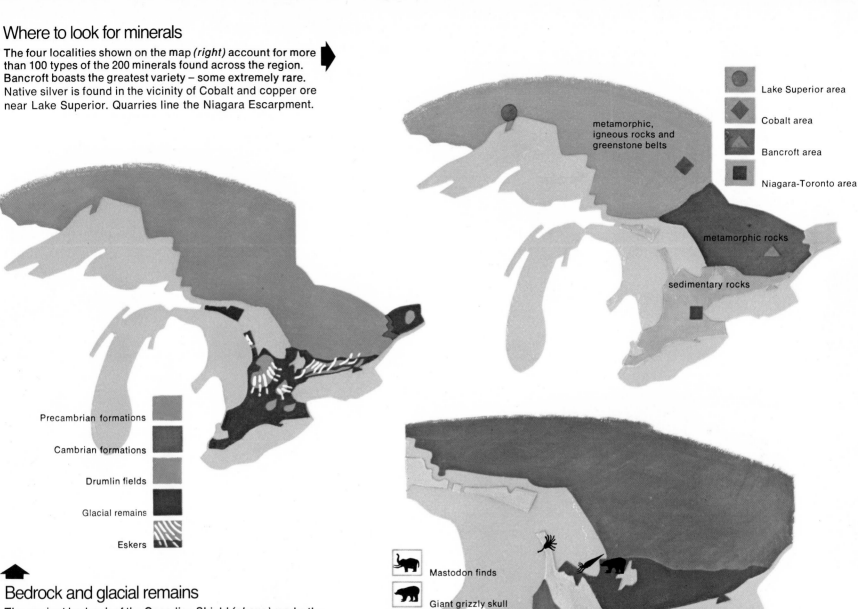

Where to look for minerals

The four localities shown on the map *(right)* account for more than 100 types of the 200 minerals found across the region. Bancroft boasts the greatest variety – some extremely rare. Native silver is found in the vicinity of Cobalt and copper ore near Lake Superior. Quarries line the Niagara Escarpment.

Lake Superior area

Cobalt area

Bancroft area

Niagara-Toronto area

metamorphic, igneous rocks and greenstone belts

metamorphic rocks

sedimentary rocks

Precambrian formations

Cambrian formations

Drumlin fields

Glacial remains

Eskers

Bedrock and glacial remains

The ancient bedrock of the Canadian Shield *(above)* marks the northern limit of the Great Lakes. It dips below the deep waters of the lakes, forming a basin for numerous layers of sedimentary rock (see also map, *right*). Drumlins and eskers are reminders of the much more recent events of the Ice Age.

Sedimentary rock and fossils

The rocks of southern Ontario reveal massive sediments, laid down throughout almost 300 million years. Fossils of three geological periods (see map, *right*) witness the evolution of life in the seas. The giant grizzly bear skull (found near Lake Simcoe) and mastodon bones are of post-glacial origin.

Mastodon finds

Giant grizzly skull

Devonian formations

Silurian formations

Ordovician formations

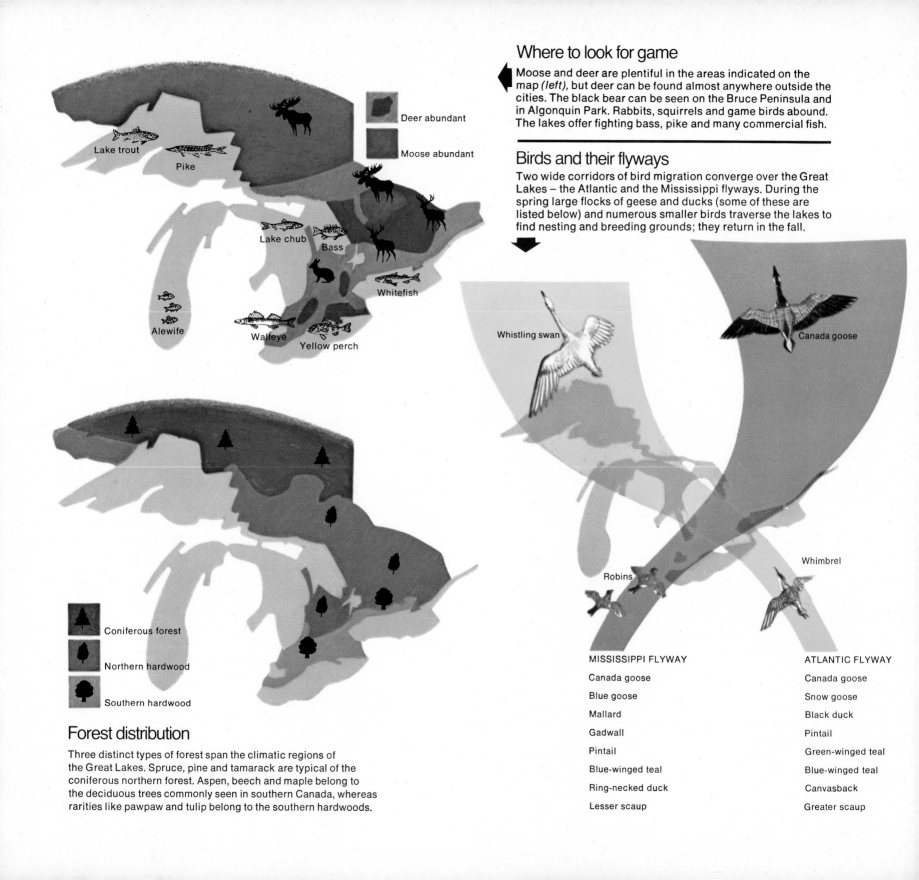

Where to look for game

Moose and deer are plentiful in the areas indicated on the map *(left)*, but deer can be found almost anywhere outside the cities. The black bear can be seen on the Bruce Peninsula and in Algonquin Park. Rabbits, squirrels and game birds abound. The lakes offer fighting bass, pike and many commercial fish.

Birds and their flyways

Two wide corridors of bird migration converge over the Great Lakes – the Atlantic and the Mississippi flyways. During the spring large flocks of geese and ducks (some of these are listed below) and numerous smaller birds traverse the lakes to find nesting and breeding grounds; they return in the fall.

Deer abundant

Moose abundant

Lake trout

Pike

Lake chub

Bass

Whitefish

Alewife

Walleye

Yellow perch

Whistling swan

Canada goose

Whimbrel

Robins

Coniferous forest

Northern hardwood

Southern hardwood

Forest distribution

Three distinct types of forest span the climatic regions of the Great Lakes. Spruce, pine and tamarack are typical of the coniferous northern forest. Aspen, beech and maple belong to the deciduous trees commonly seen in southern Canada, whereas rarities like pawpaw and tulip belong to the southern hardwoods.

MISSISSIPPI FLYWAY	ATLANTIC FLYWAY
Canada goose	Canada goose
Blue goose	Snow goose
Mallard	Black duck
Gadwall	Pintail
Pintail	Green-winged teal
Blue-winged teal	Blue-winged teal
Ring-necked duck	Canvasback
Lesser scaup	Greater scaup

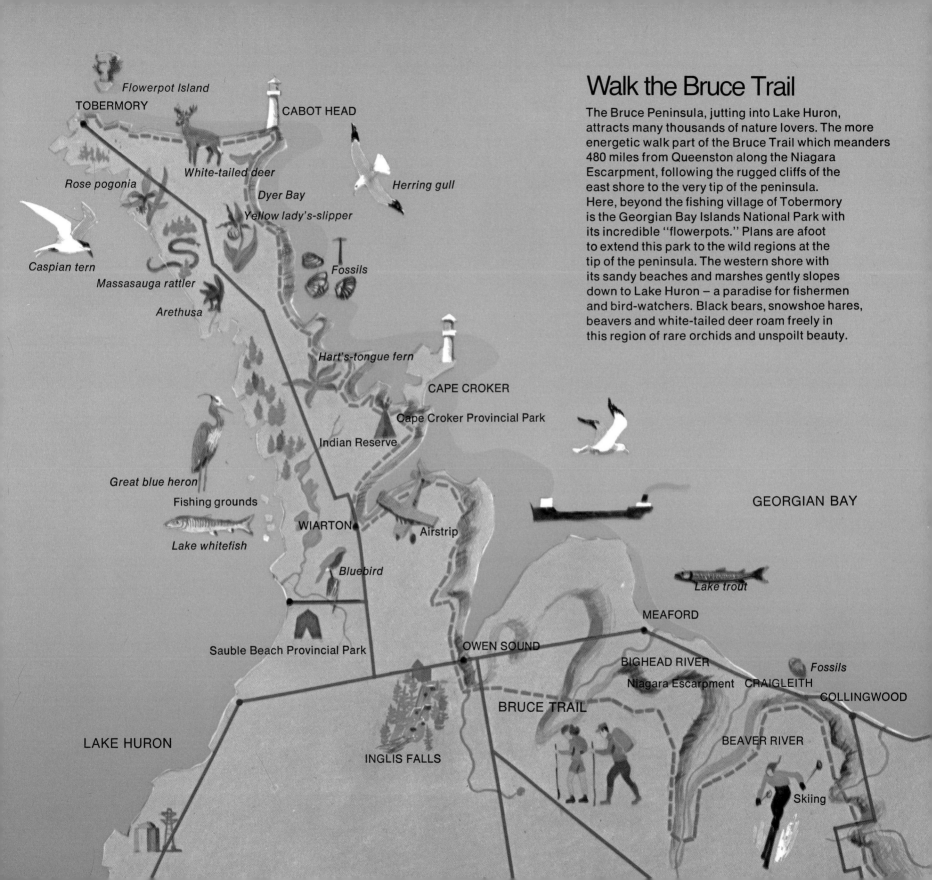

Walk the Bruce Trail

The Bruce Peninsula, jutting into Lake Huron, attracts many thousands of nature lovers. The more energetic walk part of the Bruce Trail which meanders 480 miles from Queenston along the Niagara Escarpment, following the rugged cliffs of the east shore to the very tip of the peninsula. Here, beyond the fishing village of Tobermory is the Georgian Bay Islands National Park with its incredible "flowerpots." Plans are afoot to extend this park to the wild regions at the tip of the peninsula. The western shore with its sandy beaches and marshes gently slopes down to Lake Huron – a paradise for fishermen and bird-watchers. Black bears, snowshoe hares, beavers and white-tailed deer roam freely in this region of rare orchids and unspoilt beauty.

Flowerpot Island

TOBERMORY

CABOT HEAD

White-tailed deer

Rose pogonia

Dyer Bay

Herring gull

Yellow lady's-slipper

Caspian tern

Massasauga rattler

Fossils

Arethusa

Hart's-tongue fern

CAPE CROKER

Cape Croker Provincial Park

Indian Reserve

GEORGIAN BAY

Great blue heron

Fishing grounds

WIARTON

Airstrip

Lake whitefish

Bluebird

Lake trout

MEAFORD

Sauble Beach Provincial Park

OWEN SOUND

BIGHEAD RIVER

Fossils

Niagara Escarpment   CRAIGLEITH

COLLINGWOOD

BRUCE TRAIL

LAKE HURON

BEAVER RIVER

INGLIS FALLS

Skiing

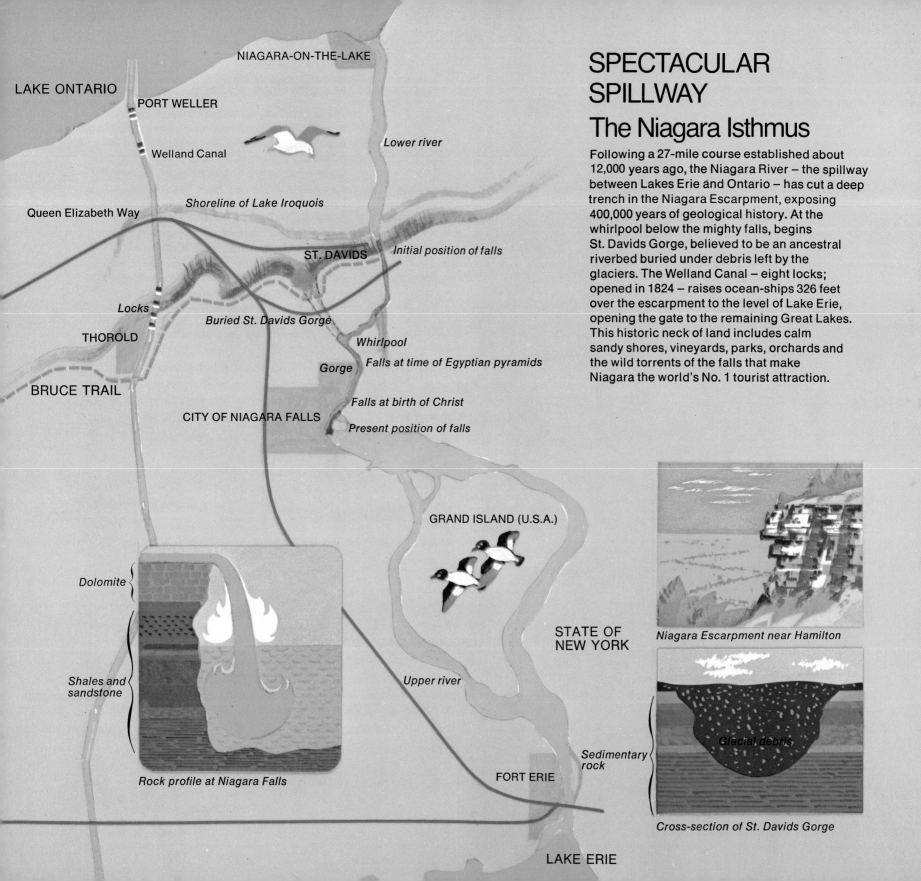

SPECTACULAR SPILLWAY
The Niagara Isthmus

Following a 27-mile course established about 12,000 years ago, the Niagara River – the spillway between Lakes Erie and Ontario – has cut a deep trench in the Niagara Escarpment, exposing 400,000 years of geological history. At the whirlpool below the mighty falls, begins St. Davids Gorge, believed to be an ancestral riverbed buried under debris left by the glaciers. The Welland Canal – eight locks; opened in 1824 – raises ocean-ships 326 feet over the escarpment to the level of Lake Erie, opening the gate to the remaining Great Lakes. This historic neck of land includes calm sandy shores, vineyards, parks, orchards and the wild torrents of the falls that make Niagara the world's No. 1 tourist attraction.

Niagara Escarpment near Hamilton

Cross-section of St. Davids Gorge

Rock profile at Niagara Falls

PART ONE / **THE REGION**

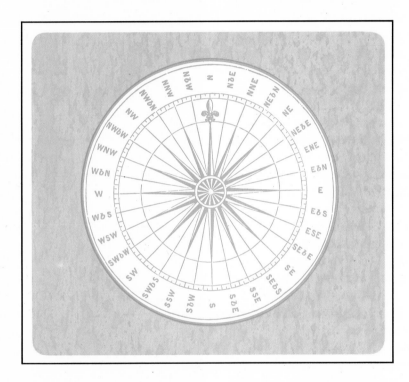

1 THE AQUATIC DOMAIN

Statistics about the size of the Great Lakes almost always give a distorted picture. The reader is left with the feeling that the lakes are in some way an interruption to the land. But they are a world in themselves, with their own life, climate, history, destiny and regions. Even the number of five Great Lakes is misleading. The North Channel between Manitoulin Island and the mainland, for instance, isn't included in the number, yet this is a 150-mile reach of islands and broken shoreline. Georgian Bay is fragmented into tens of thousands of islands, bays, straits and channels. Its east shoreline is like the edge of a piece of lace.

There are as many different lakes as there are points of view. Seen from the deck of a ship coming out of the St. Lawrence into Lake Ontario, where the shore suddenly falls away to a streak of powder blue on the horizon, and the white caps march in across bands of emerald green and deep blue water, the lakes are a remote and barren expanse, more monotonous than the desert. Usually there is no sign of life out on the lakes except perhaps a lone ring-billed gull resting on the waves.

Yet you can lie in a skiff anchored off a peaceful headland on Georgian Bay looking over the shady side of the boat into a patch of lake bottom no bigger than a front lawn and peer down into a sunny jungle of aquatic life. Bass cruise by like green submarines. Sunfish flash like space ships hovering over a forest. Schools of minnows pass in tight regimental formation, changing course on some mysterious command.

The character of the lakes depends on the focus. A glass of water dipped from deep water looks as clear as drinking water. Yet when a few gallons have been strained through a nylon net, and the net rinsed down into a small glass jar, the water is tinted bright green with a cloud of wriggling forms that, under a magnifying glass, appear in a multitude of bizarre shapes. The surface of the lake is a busy threshold between two worlds. In parts of the lakes in early summer the whole surface seems to blossom.

A gentle breeze ripples Lake Superior below the cliffs of Thunder Bay. Fed by 200 rivers, it is the world's largest freshwater lake.

Around the islands at the west end of Lake Erie, burrowing and stone-clinging insects that have matured on the lake bottom rise to the surface, perform gymnastics of metamorphosis, change into air-borne creatures and stream out like plumes of smoke toward the land to live out their lives between sunrise and sunset. In the spring the plant life in the water blooms. Water temperatures become uniform from top to bottom and the entire lake turns over, as its surface is stirred by spring breezes. Vertical currents take oxygen down to the countless inhabitants of the lake bottoms. The salts and minerals of the lake water are mixed as uniformly as if they were being stirred in a chemist's beaker. The water smells of fresh growth.

In winter, the lakes are a scene of desolation. Blocks of ice, rammed up over one another by the waves, form a barrier along the shore. In the west end of Lake Ontario the cobalt-blue water is dotted with brilliant white ice floes that have broken loose from the Niagara River. On cold mornings, steam-fog as thick as shaving lather lies over the leaden-coloured lakes, carried upward by the slightest air movement into fantastic twists and curlicues and spikes. Occasionally a research ship goes out onto the lakes in winter, breaking through the ice of the harbour. The ice up-ends around the prow in enormous green-edged sheets about eight inches thick. It is a common occurrence to see land birds stuck in the ice near the shore. From the deck of the ship, men reach out with poles and break up the ice around the birds, which then seem able to work themselves loose. But out in the middle of the lake, the ship moves through a strangely soft world. You can feel the warmth of the water, which acts as a great thermostat. There is snow on the deck, but it is melting.

The Great Lakes have changed enormously since the first Europeans paddled along their waterways trying to reach China, California, the Gulf of Mexico, Eldorado. Just about everything worth reaching, they believed, lay at the end of the Great Lakes. It is a sad experience today to approach the lake shore through, say, a parking lot in Port Credit, and stand beside a depressed-looking weeping willow, or embattled sooty clump of golden rod, and look across a lake margin of malted milk cartons, tins, a patch of purple oil slick, and see the lakes lying as if asphyxiated beneath a pall of factory smoke.

The lakes have become polluted in all built-up areas. Yet, away from the activities of man, they are much the same as they

19

have always been. Lake Superior has hardly changed at all. Father Claude Allouez, describing Lake Superior in the *Jesuit Relations* of 1668, wrote ". . . the water is so clear and pure that objects at the bottom can be seen to the depths of six brasses" (36 feet). This is exactly the reading obtained today on a secchi disc, a white metal plate that is lowered into the water by a thin cable. The depth at which the disc disappears is the measure of the water's transparency.

The greatest change in the lakes has taken place around the St. Clair and Detroit Rivers, the west end of Lake Erie, and the Hamilton-Toronto region of Lake Ontario (and the cities on the American side). Mrs. Simcoe referred to the "crystal clear waters" of Toronto Bay, which is now so polluted that it doesn't even smell like water. Henry Rowe Schoolcraft, a geologist and Indian agent for the U.S. Government, wrote of the Detroit in 1820: "The river is broad and deep with gravelly shore and transparent water . . ." Today in this region a pure white secchi disc lowered into the water under a bright noon sun, disappears two and a half feet beneath the surface. But even here, the clear water of Lake Huron tends to go right down the centre of the Detroit, and the middle of the river is relatively pure. Nature struggles to preserve herself amid man's destructive activities.

2 THE BALMY SOUTH

In the extreme southwest corner of the Great Lakes a finger of land extends farther south than any other part of Canada. Coming down the Detroit River in a lake boat is like floating through the savannas of Texas, and it would not be hard to imagine bison coming down to the shore to drink. The river comes out in a kind of Caribbean of warm shallow waters and low islands at the west end of Lake Erie. It's a soft, beachy, watery domain where the land and the lakes seem to have come to a friendly compromise. There are deltas at the mouth of the St. Clair River and meadows a few inches above the lake level. Turtles cross the highways. The headlands of Lake Erie are so low on the water that on a hazy day it's hard to tell where the land ends and the water begins. The whole shore of Lake Erie is a mild, flat farming region. Coming into, say, Port Stanley on

Lake Erie in a lake boat on a summer evening when the shad flies fill the air, and driving up through the flat farm lands of water melon, sugar beets, sweet corn and tobacco, which extend flat and serene in all directions, gives the feeling that this is a remote southern coast of Canada. Silver poplars shed their fuzzy-backed leaves along the old beach roads. Opossums climb the hackberry trees, and cactus grows on the sand pits. The land is low and possibly because of this you get the feeling – standing, perhaps, on the south tip of Point Pelee, looking out over the green combers coming in from the horizon – that these Great Lakes are really inland seas which might come up and inundate the land, as they did throughout much of the region's geological history.

At the opposite end of Lake Erie, the feeling of serenity and ancient balance between land and water ends abruptly. The beaches, the gentle sloping shoreline, are gone. The Great Lakes enter a region of rock and roaring water. The Niagara River which drains Lake Erie begins as a wide, peaceful stream flowing between green parklands but, as it splits around Grand Island, it races north as if overcome by a kind of hysteria, towards a cloud of mist.

Coming up to the falls on the Canadian side, you can look across the outlet for all the upper lakes without seeing water at all. There is nothing ahead but a rock wall, with people and traffic moving on the other side. But the earth trembles. A roar fills the air. When you come up to the brink you look down on gulls wheeling above slowly swirling green water. The wind from the falls drives the mist up from below, soaking rock ledges and grass and plants at the edge of the gorge. It's an awesome spectacle, and nervous viewers, coming to the guard rail to get their first look, edge uneasily back from the sight.

The falls drop over rocks that were laid down on the bottom of the sea some 400 million years ago. The ridge over which the falls drop is the Niagara Escarpment, created by the normal continuing processes of erosion that began when the entire region was a stark, lifeless land, recently freed from the seas. All this happened over the last 300 million years. But in "recent" times, that is, in time measured in less than a million years, this ridge was overridden by glaciers that covered the region with ice a mile thick. When the glaciers pulled back from the area for the last time and the falls began to drop over the ridge and cut Niagara Gorge, man had reached North America from Asia. This was not long before written history began. The falls had existed only about 6,000 years before the time of the building of the Egyptian pyramids.

The Niagara Escarpment, which creates the falls, is a giant, apparently irrelevant step in the earth's surface that runs along the south shore of Lake Ontario, sheltering the vineyards and peach groves of the Niagara Peninsula. In this section the escarpment is an almost featureless wall of land with occasional picturesque waterfalls. In the region of Collingwood, on the south shore of Georgian Bay, the escarpment rises to over 1,700 feet. At its top, beds of dolomite form sheer grey cliffs, beneath which are slumped blocks forming sheltered environments, locally referred to as "caves." Snow and ice persist in these sheltered areas until mid-summer. The escarpment divides southern Ontario in half and forms the major land features throughout the region. If you drive west from Toronto along Highway 401, you pass a promontory of its rock face in the vicinity of Campbellville. This promontory appears as a step on the horizon that can be seen for thirty miles or more. The escarpment is not an unbroken ridge. Big notches in it accommodate the cities of Hamilton and Owen Sound, and there are areas where it seems to dip beneath the hills of southern Ontario.

3 THE GLACIAL HILLS

North from the shore of Lake Ontario, the land climbs into hilly terrain. The glaciers that advanced over this land thousands of years ago moulded and streamlined the surface deposits of sand and clay, giving the land the appearance of a great rumpled green rug. In some areas the hills converge into rolling country. Just east of Cobourg on Highway 401, there is a dense concentration of these hills – drumlins. At night they loom in flowing black shapes along the highway, like a silent school of whales following the traffic. But often there'll be one solitary hill in the middle of a farmer's field, streamlined as if some sculptor accidentally dropped a piece of modelling material and reached down and smoothed it with his hand as he went

DRUMLIN FIELDS
Wherever glaciers advanced over the land, drumlins were likely to form. These low hills of gravels and clay characterize Ontario's Beaver Valley and also occur in large concentrations around Peterborough and Guelph. Usually drop-shaped, they were left behind by the retreating ice about 10,000 years ago.

by, perhaps with grain fields or pasture lands flowing over it.

From Cobourg west to the vicinity of the Niagara Escarpment there is an enormous swelling of land without any rocky face or outcrops, called Oak Ridges. Every road leading north from the lake shore runs into this band of hills. A well more than 600 feet deep has been sunk here without hitting bedrock. The villages of Dagmar, Albion and Palgrave are set among these hills called moraines.

Hills appear throughout most of the central Great Lakes area that extends from the sandy beaches and dunes of Lake Huron to the head of the St. Lawrence. West of the escarpment the region slants gently southwest through some of the richest agricultural areas in Canada, over a gentle arch that centres around the city of London. But on the east the escarpment drops sharply to the low plains along the shore of Lake Ontario. For mile after mile in the Hamilton-Toronto region the shoreline is almost hidden behind gas tanks, parking lots, acres of railway sidings and expressways.

Yet there are spectacularly beautiful stretches of shoreline. Two are within the city limits of Toronto. The Scarborough Bluffs can be seen from a small park in the east end of Toronto, reached by turning south from Kingston Road at Midland Avenue. The district is a midway of shopping plazas, motels and hamburger stands, yet when you reach the shore it's like coming out on the mountains of the moon. Waves have cut the clay and sand cliffs deposited by an ancient river delta into fantastic spires and steeples. In places, they seem to hang like folds of curtains. The materials eroded by wave action from the Scarborough Bluffs drifted westward with the lake currents, and over the centuries formed a sand spit that sent tongues licking up into the bay between the spit and the mainland. This was the origin of the Toronto Islands, which lie off-shore directly opposite the centre of the city. In 1852 waves broke through the spit. Other storms cut into it until today there's an archipelago of fifteen islands nestling within a four-mile hook. It's a quiet, restful, willow-draped meeting-place of land and water, disappearing fast under the pressure of population and formal parklands.

At the east end of Lake Ontario, a peninsula of 390 square miles extends twenty-five miles south of the main line of the shore, almost entirely cut off by the Bay of Quinte. The shoreline seems to have completely forgotten in what direction it is going or any desire to get there. The whole region is a surpassingly beautiful rural Venice. Long reaches and sounds form a lazy pattern throughout the peninsula. The elms on the distant shores look as though they were rooted on the surface of the water. There are a few formations along the roads, where the

HOW TORONTO ISLANDS WERE MADE

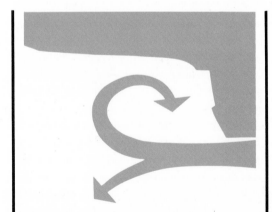

Eroded sand from the high cliffs at Scarborough was carried by easterly currents (in the direction of the arrows) *and dumped off the site of present-day Toronto.*

In 1858 a storm severed the sand-bar near the eastern end of the peninsula (above, right) *which, by then, had enclosed Toronto Bay; thus the fickle shoal turned into an island.*

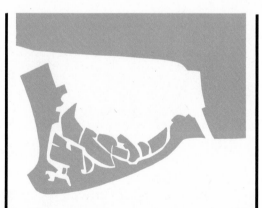

Further developed by man, the islands take this shape today. A four-mile city parkland, with exotic trees in children's playgrounds, they now attract many thousands of visitors.

rocks are arranged in neat layers as though laid for a fireplace, but the region is generally green, flat, and in places, marshy. In the southwestern part of the peninsula there's a spectacular region of high sand dunes. These are active shifting dunes, that will form a four- or five-foot ridge around a shack on the shore in a couple of seasons. The tips of buried trees protrude from them and in some areas they form towering bowls of fine sand with rims so sharp they look as though they'd collapse if you laid a teaspoon on them.

Near the docks of the car ferry that connects with the highway to Adolphustown, there's a lake up on the top of a hill, called "Lake on the Mountain". The shores are at road level, but on the other side of the road you look down on a vista of the Bay of Quinte, a land that appears like a flood area, far below. The imagination jumps to a picture of water mysteriously coming uphill to fill the lake and there is a spooky local legend that it comes directly from Lake Erie, 150 miles away, without dropping over Niagara Falls. Observations made by skindivers have dispelled this notion. The illusion is due to the fact that the waters which supply the lake flow between layers of limestone from ground higher than the lake, but from sources so distant that a spectator, standing on the shore of the lake, doesn't take them into account.

Lake on the Mountain, a natural curiosity, suggests the illusion of water flowing uphill – but it is fed by underground streams.

4 THE MEETING WITH THE SHIELD

There is a feeling, driving up Highway 11 north of Barrie, that some major event is pending, that nature is in a kind of suspension. There are a few rocky pastures and hayfields, but the big rolling farmlands have disappeared. There are no more neatly shaped wooded lots surrounded by green fields. The bush that borders the road is continuous for long stretches. Just north of Orillia on the west side of the highway, a patch of pink rock the size of a front porch breaks smoothly through the topsoil, the first outpost of a new kind of rock that will appear farther north as massive blocks the size of apartment buildings.

This is the southern border of the Canadian Shield, and the Great Lakes drainage basin laps up onto it throughout this area. The shield covers a vast region to the north of the lakes. This mass of hard dense rock was formed between one and three billion years ago. The edge of the shield skirts the northeastern tip of Lake Ontario and it runs almost due west till it meets Lake Huron on Georgian Bay. It is covered by the waters of this bay along the Northern Channel of Lake Huron. The shield describes a wide arc under the southeastern shore of Lake Superior down into the Green Bay area of Wisconsin.

In southern Ontario you come to this zone along any highway running north or east from the lake shores, and you can put your finger on it at the Kingston interchange between Highways 15 and 401. You strike it driving from Toronto to Ottawa. Suddenly you're out of farmlands and in a rugged region of massive rock. The Kawartha Lakes, spilling into one another from their sides, zig-zag along the edge of the shield with Lake Simcoe forming an anchor point.

The shore of Georgian Bay is reached only through certain points, such as Honey Harbour, Parry Sound, Byng Inlet, and through bush or by water. Killarney Provincial Park is reached by Highway 637, that clambers over and around rocks the size of tennis courts through more than forty miles of solid bush, to come out on a shoreline fragmented into a maze of low, pink rock islands. The shores of Lake Superior in some places are sheer cliffs of shield rock that drop eight hundred feet into the water, although along most of these shores there's a thin ribbon of white sand at the base of the rocks that would take some minor mountain climbing to reach.

Stretches of Highway 17 wind and roll along this kind of shore from Batchawana Bay through Lake Superior Provincial Park to Michipicoten. One of the most spectacular stretches of the Canadian Pacific transcontinental railway route skirts the lake between Heron Bay and Port Arthur. In places the track is hewn out of the solid rock of the shoreline and presents a virtually sheer drop to the clear waters below. At the Lakehead, Mount McKay and the Sleeping Giant loom above this land of ancient rock, looking like left-overs from a forgotten mountain range.

The Great Lakes and Ottawa Valley drainage basins meet in Algonquin Park, a 2,900-square-mile provincial preserve, located in the southern part of this Canadian Shield, amid the kind of sombre, worn-down mountains painted by the Canadian artists J. E. H. Macdonald and Arthur Lismer. They're covered with forests, but in places the rock thrusts through the thin soil in great blocks and flowing surfaces. This is a vastly different land from the cultivated regions of southern Ontario. The very feeling is different. Often you can't see the ground beyond the nearest rock which forms a horizon thirty or forty feet away, with just the tops of poplars and birches visible beyond it. Some of these rocks form a wide stone pavement, so nearly flat that

The total drainage area of the Great Lakes – 288,770 square miles – could contain almost all of France and Great Britain combined.

you could bicycle on them. The rocks are stained with mosses and low fuzzy shrubs that manage to cling to soil so shallow that a spade driven into it whangs against rock as though striking the core of the earth, which in a sense the rock in this region is. Rivers are black slots through solid rock walls and the bush is laced with lakes.

Instructions put out by the Government of Ontario for a canoe trip give an idea of what the terrain is like. "The starting-point of this route is above the dam on the northeast channel of Canoe Lake at the foot of Joe Lake. Proceed northerly about one mile, then follow the easterly arm of Joe Lake and enter Little Joe Lake; thence to the northerly tip of Little Joe Lake to a small stream; proceed upstream to a portage; portage about 600 yards to Baby Joe Lake then to a 200-yard portage leading to Burnt Island Lake; proceed through Burnt Island Lake to a portage midway along its northeasterly shore; portage about 900 yards to the southwesterly bay of Little Otterslide Lake; proceed to the most northerly narrows of Little Otterslide Lake; thence northerly through the westerly bay of Otterslide Lake to a portage; proceed northerly over a series of portages and small unnamed lakes and streams to Big Trout Lake . . ." There are nearly two pages of instructions like this, and reading them one begins to get an idea of the kind of route followed by the explorers and fur traders who came through this tongue of the shield on their way to the upper lakes and the west.

An even better way to get something of the feeling of what it was like to open up this country is to take a walk along one of the nature trails in the park in summer. It's rough work, clambering up rock faces and carefully stepping around the edges of bogs, under fierce attack by black flies and mosquitoes, torn between a desire to read all the fascinating stories told on the plaques that are posted on the trees by park naturalists describing the nature of the region, and the urge to get out of the bush.

Father Gabriel Sagard, a Recollet friar, who crossed this country in 1623, described the mosquitoes and black flies that have tormented fishermen and campers in this part of the world ever since. "If I had not kept my face wrapped in a cloth, I am almost sure they would have blinded me, so pestiferous and poisonous are the bites of these little demons . . . I confess that this is the worst martyrdom I suffered in this country: hunger, thirst, weariness and fever are nothing to it."

An ice crystal of fairytale delicacy – but still the basic unit of the merciless glacier.

HOW GLACIERS MADE THE LAKES

Awesome glaciers often two miles high clasped the continent in an icy grip, sweeping all life before them, crushing mountain ranges and scooping out the basins for the Great Lakes.

Anatomy of the glacier

When the temperature on the earth's surface cools by just a few degrees, the water evaporating from the oceans accumulates increasingly as snow in high northern mountain valleys; the frigid climate there prevents melting and the snow is compressed into a solid mass of ice, thousands of feet thick. In an ice age – there may have been many of them in the earth's long history – the ice spills across the earth's crust as viscous liquid, tears down the tops of mountains, gouges valleys smooth, and rasps the surface of plains with its embedded debris like sandpaper on wood. Under increasing pressure from the central dome the glacier spreads, relentlessly razing the ground – like some insatiable monster. After thousands of years the temperature gradually rises – for reasons yet unknown. Fissures in the glacier's surface deepen, crevasses widen and boulders and rubble are disgorged. At the margin, or "snout" of the glacier piles of rubble form neat mounds called end moraines. Over the past million years, during the Pleistocene epoch, this process has repeated itself at least four times. The undulating land and its rich soil surrounding the lakes owe their origin to the Wisconsin, the last of the "ice monsters" which retreated only a mere 10,000 years ago.

Snowflakes

Modified snowflakes

Compacted granular snow

This diagram shows the transition from snow to ice within a fifty-foot section of the glacier.

The arrows indicate flow of rubble contained within the glacier along faults in the ice, forming moraines at the "snout" of the glacier.

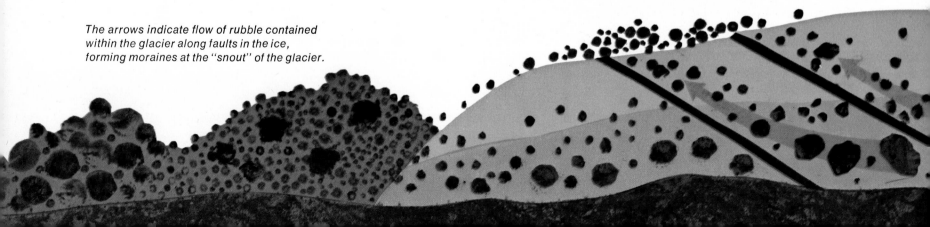

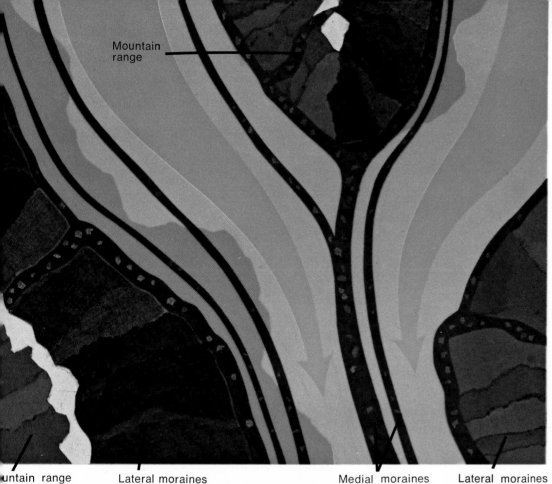

Mountain range

Mountain range   Lateral moraines   Medial moraines   Lateral moraines

Rivers of ice

Measurements show that ice along the centre of existing glaciers can flow more than 150 feet per day. During its advance down a valley the glacier plucks fragments from the rockbed, to gouge a broad, even, U-shaped channel, unlike the meandering V-shaped bed of a mountain stream. Streams of rubble carried along at the outer margins of the ice sheet are known as lateral moraines. Like streams, glaciers have their tributaries and where two valleys meet (see illustration at left) the lateral moraines closest to the centre join to form a medial moraine. The number of medial moraines within a glacier indicate how many valleys have contributed to its formation.

Below: Seventeen Ottawa Peace Towers – each 300 feet high – stacked one on top of the other, give some idea of the depth of ice bearing down during the period of glaciation.

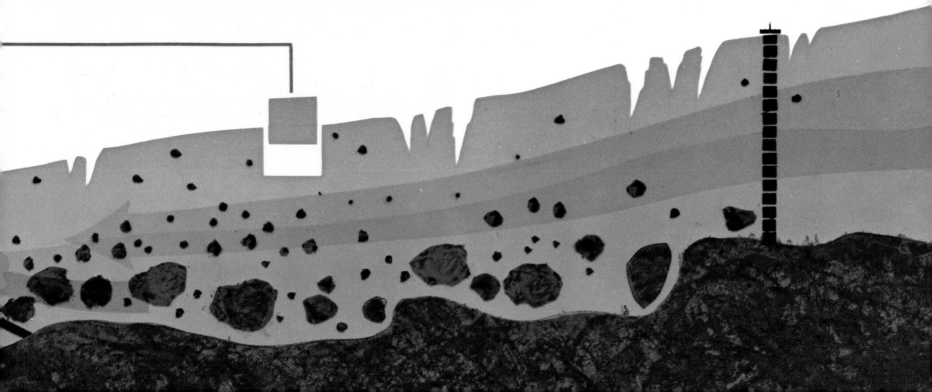

Vultures

Smilodon

Spruce trees

Advance of the Wisconsin Glacier

Less than 20,000 years ago, glaciers were still advancing across the North American continent, obliterating everything that had taken root during the unexplained intervening periods. This artist's portrayal concentrates some of the large animals existing at the time into a small area – feeding among the dwindling vegetation of hardy pines and birch trees. A ferocious sabre-toothed tiger, the smilodon, could have lurked in wait for the 14-foot-high mammoth, while a giant vulture hovered overhead. Powerful ground sloths, the size of an elephant, survived until man's arrival. Large beavers, whose tail alone measured three feet, made matchwood of the trees. Peccaries, forerunners of today's pigs, and native horses roamed open grassy spaces. Of all the animals shown the only one that has survived to the present day is the muskox (in foreground at right).

Giant beaver

Woolly mammoth

Ground sloth

Glacier advancing

Pine tree

Peccaries

Horses

Birch trees

Muskox

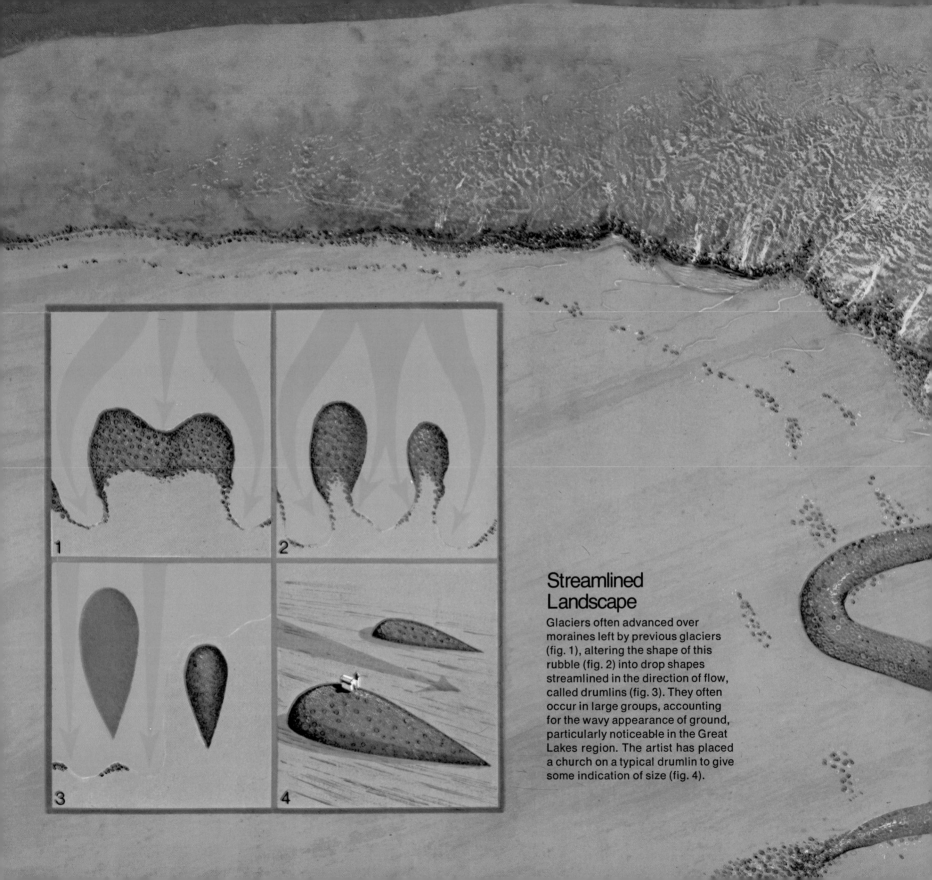

Streamlined Landscape

Glaciers often advanced over moraines left by previous glaciers (fig. 1), altering the shape of this rubble (fig. 2) into drop shapes streamlined in the direction of flow, called drumlins (fig. 3). They often occur in large groups, accounting for the wavy appearance of ground, particularly noticeable in the Great Lakes region. The artist has placed a church on a typical drumlin to give some indication of size (fig. 4).

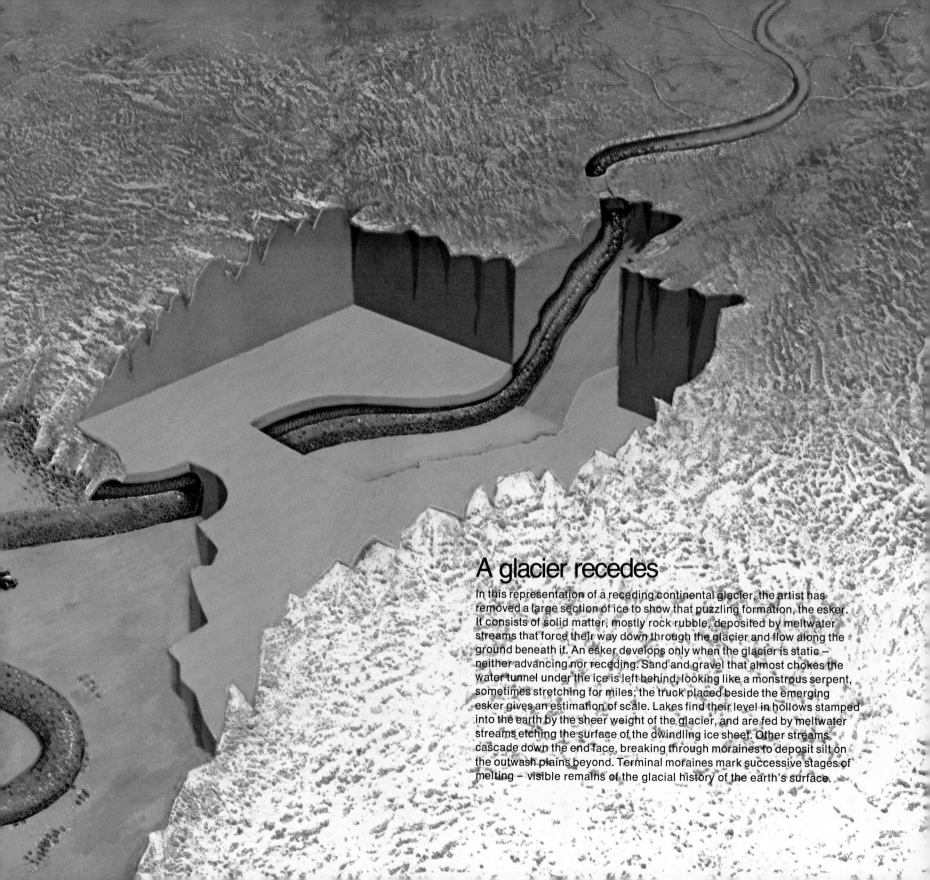

A glacier recedes

In this representation of a receding continental glacier, the artist has removed a large section of ice to show that puzzling formation, the esker. It consists of solid matter, mostly rock rubble, deposited by meltwater streams that force their way down through the glacier and flow along the ground beneath it. An esker develops only when the glacier is static – neither advancing nor receding. Sand and gravel that almost chokes the water tunnel under the ice is left behind, looking like a monstrous serpent, sometimes stretching for miles; the truck placed beside the emerging esker gives an estimation of scale. Lakes find their level in hollows stamped into the earth by the sheer weight of the glacier, and are fed by meltwater streams etching the surface of the dwindling ice sheet. Other streams cascade down the end face, breaking through moraines to deposit silt on the outwash plains beyond. Terminal moraines mark successive stages of melting – visible remains of the glacial history of the earth's surface.

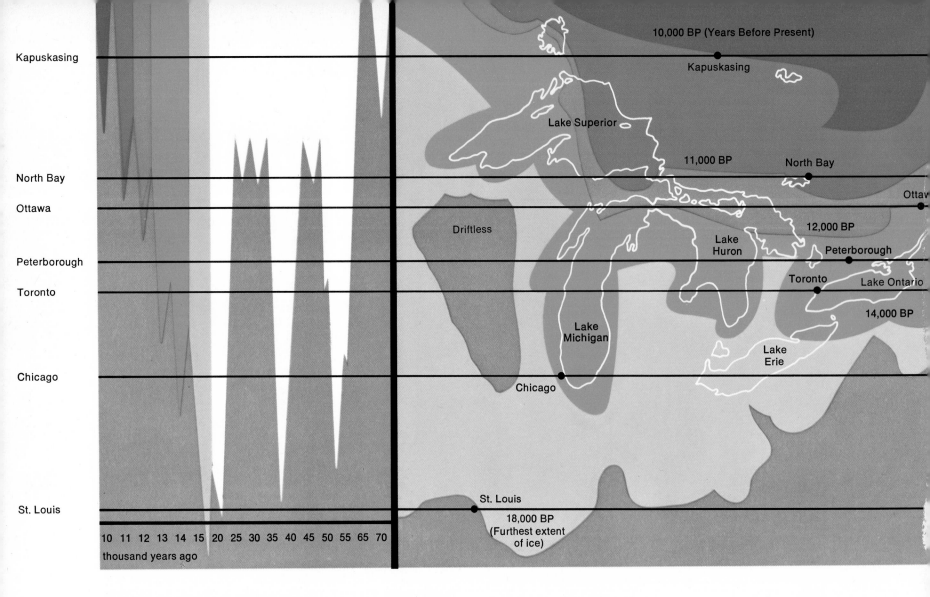

Kapuskasing

North Bay

Ottawa

Peterborough

Toronto

Chicago

St. Louis

10 11 12 13 14 15 20 25 30 35 40 45 50 55 65 70

thousand years ago

10,000 BP (Years Before Present)
Kapuskasing

Lake Superior

11,000 BP   North Bay

Ottaw

Driftless   12,000 BP

Lake
Huron   Peterborough

Toronto   Lake Ontario

14,000 BP

Lake
Michigan

Lake
Erie

Chicago

St. Louis

18,000 BP
(Furthest extent
of ice)

Wisconsin glacial period

The chart above summarizes the extent of
glaciation during the Wisconsin glacier
period, about 65,000 years. We may now be
living in an interglacial period, but
how and when the next ice age is going
to announce itself no one knows.

End of the last ice age

The most recent ice sheet to cover the Great Lakes region reached its peak 18,000 years
ago. Massive fingers of the Wisconsin glacier retreated and then came back again
across the land. Over the next 5,000 years, the ice fought a losing battle with the warmer
climate (as shown on the map above). Vast lakes at the margins of the melting ice spilled
into outlets to the sea—whence, in the great cycle of nature, the glacier ice had originated.
The earth was in flux: freed from the ice, it rebounded, constantly changing lake levels
and margins, moulding them to their present shape.

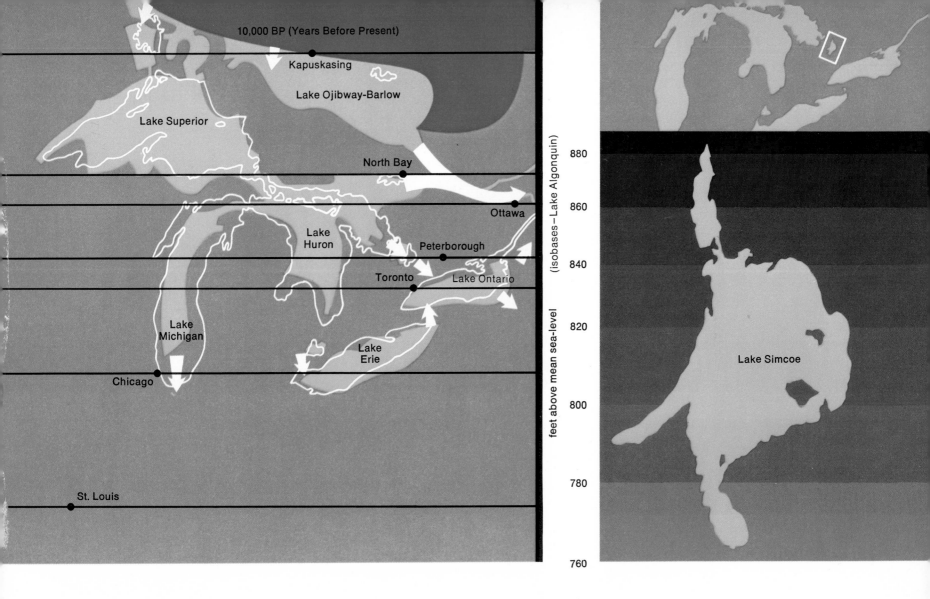

The lakes take shape

The expanse of water appearing to the north of the Great Lakes (as they looked 10,000 years ago) is Lake Ojibway-Barlow. It was formed by the meltwater of the receding Wisconsin ice-sheet. The dark arrows indicate the direction of the drainage over the last 10,000 years. The silt deposited in Lake Ojibway-Barlow covered the rocky Shield and left a 400 mile strip of the Shield fertile, near today's Kapuskasing.

The land rebounds

Released from its overburden of ice, the earth's crust springs back, like a ball bouncing in extremely slow motion. The surface of a watershed is a convenient gauge of this recoil, known as differential uplift. The north shore of Lake Simcoe (see area outlined at top) is rising above the south shore at the rate of about one foot per century. This tilt is plotted in colour graduations on the diagram.

Spruce trees growing on receding glacier

Esker

Deer

Bear

Dire wolf

Muskox with calf

Recession of the Wisconsin Glacier

Gradually, life flowed north again, in the wake of the receding glaciers. When the Wisconsin finally succumbed to the warmer climate, and the Great Lakes began to take their present shape, the region looked much as the tundra of the North does today. Hunters from Asia had penetrated the area to kill off the last of the cervalces, a type of fallow deer with antlers ten feet wide, related to the Irish elk. Mastodons, the largest land mammal to survive the ice age, browsed on the spruce trees that took root even on ice. These elephantine creatures became extinct only 8,000 years ago. Packs of dire wolves (see specimen in foreground, left) roamed the barren land, but natural selection favoured the slightly larger timber wolf. Bears, muskox, deer and many other species living today had already become well established by this time.

Cervalces

Spruce trees

Mastodon

The Axel Heiberg glacier, high in the Canadian Arctic, is all that remains today of the Wisconsin. This aerial view shows a glacial lake hemmed in by ice and the outwash plain is visible in the far distance behind the ice.

PART TWO / GEOLOGY

5 THE FORMING OF THE ROCKS

When the Great Lakes region began to take shape, about 600 million years ago, the story of the continent was already an old story. For thousands of millions of years, its now-exposed rocks had been warped and melted, ejected from volcanoes, squeezed through fissures, sand-blasted by desert winds, covered by oceans and even by ice. These rocks are among the oldest known geological formations on the American continent. The oldest originated about 2,500 million years ago. The rugged landscape of the Muskoka-Haliburton region is all that remains of an ancient mountain range, whose peaks may have been higher than the Rockies a billion years ago. Wind and water have planed them down to their very roots.

Many different types of rock have contributed to produce the massive rock shelf known as the Canadian Shield. They all date back to the Precambrian era and have remained almost unchanged for the last 600 million years. Dipping down deep under the younger rocks, they form the basement of the earth's crust below the Great Lakes. Although stable during this time, the land was subject to gentle upheavals, perhaps the aftermath of its violent youth. Seas ebbed and flowed across its surface. Nothing broke the silence but the roar of the surf and the sound of the tide. When the tide went out it left miles of dripping mudflats. Occasionally, storms raged and lightning threw its blue flashes over the land. Perhaps on some days the sun shone with a reddish-brown light, through a pall of volcanic ash that floated across the sky from a great disturbance to the east, where the earth's crust was being thrust up to form the Appalachians.

About 450 million years ago, the limestones of the Kingston-Peterborough area were laid down. The beginning of this Ordovician rock-building can be seen at the interchange of Highways 401 and 15, and also on the southside of the side-road into Nephton, north of Lakefield. Here the contact between the ocean bottom and the shield can be seen in a rock formation about six feet high, overhung by a grassy bank. The rock layers in the outcrop are clearly of different kinds. The ones below are a smooth, gnarled, pink-and-rust-coloured mass (granite). The ones on top are cracked and crumbled sections of a fine-textured grey limestone. The ones below are the ancient rocks of the shield. The ones above are the hardened sediments laid down by seas that washed against the older rock. You can put your finger on the line between the upper and lower formations and span the time gap between two worlds 500 million years apart.

The deposition of limestone was followed by a succession of muds and sands as the sea became shallower. They hardened into the shales and sandstones of the late Ordovician period which form part of the bedrock that underlies southern Ontario. They are still visible in many places near Toronto – in the Humber Valley, along Etobicoke Creek. One of the best displays of shales laid down by these ancient seas can be seen at the Toronto Brick Company yards, where they make up the bottom sixty feet of the quarry. Situated in the Don Valley, this quarry can be seen looking north from the Bloor Street viaduct, and reached by the Bayview extension which skirts it just south of the Pottery Road turnoff.

With a further rise of the Appalachians, rivers red with mud flowed westward from the young mountains. The deltas of these rivers intermingled and sprawled over a distance of four hundred miles, from east of what is now Lake Ontario to points beyond the present shore of Lake Huron. The shale left behind by this expanse of deltas is called the Queenston formation. The rivers ran through a bald and desolate land, and were slowed down as they met the heavier sea water. Delta building continued into the Silurian period. The remains of these deltas are evident as the sandy ledge-forming rocks of the Niagara Gorge. The same sandy layers can be traced along the Niagara Escarpment to Hamilton, and in wells drilled for oil and gas, west and northwest of Niagara Falls.

Beyond the edges of the sandstone deltas the seas were clear. Limestones and other carbonate rocks, like dolomite, are the result of sedimentation on the bottom of these seas. By this time, complex forms of life had developed in these seas. Myriads of small beings built reef colonies – very much like the coral reefs of the Caribbean Sea and the Pacific Islands existing today. Many of the Silurian reef-building organisms, called *stromatoporoids*, are now extinct.

Corals and tiny fantastically shaped marine animals, some with the appearance of plants and flowers, some looking like miniature sheaves of wheat, lived around or inside skeletons that they built from the lime of the seawater. They cemented themselves together in enormous colonies that formed high, honeycombed columns – coral reefs – and breached the water as grey or white shoals in the troughs of the waves. Present day reef-building organisms live only in clear water, and the same was probably true in the distant past. Eventually the Silurian seas in the Great Lakes area became crystal clear, and reef-building spread through large areas of the water, unhampered by delta formation. Lockport dolomite, the cap-rock of the Niagara Escarpment, was largely a product of this process. This same rock unit also acts as host rock for the oil and gas tapped in southwestern Ontario.

Other rock formations resulting from this reef-building phase of the past can be seen on the Bruce Peninsula, often forming irregular outcrops of dolomite or limestone, light grey in colour and uniform in structure. Manitoulin Island is a direct continuation of these formations, separated only by a shallow channel from the headland of the Bruce Peninsula. Fossil reefs are frequently exposed as haphazard assemblages of rock, because when a chunk of reef was battered loose by the waves it slid into the deeper water to roll around in a jumble of debris. Sometimes it was pulverized by the motion of the water to the texture of mud. From this ground-up material a mound of fine coral sands formed at the base of the reef. It made a bed for more reef growth and a sunny haunt for shell-fish. When these sea creatures died, their shells were ground up in turn and added to the mass of the coral reef. The reef became an almost inexhaustible factory of lime that wandered in the currents to be deposited in other areas of the sea, where it was compressed and squeezed dry under its own weight. Chemical processes cemented the coral grains together and helped turn them into the solid rock.

In southwest Ontario the pattern of reef-growth gave rise to isolated lagoons in which the sea water evaporated. These pockets of water could be called the predecessors to the modern

COMMON FOSSILS

Corals and other marine animals cemented themselves together to form enormous coral reefs in the Silurian seas.

Rugose colonial coral.   *Clam-like brachiopod.*   *Pelecypod – a true clam.*   *Gastropod – a marine snail.*

Limestone deposits in the Great Lakes region are the remains of coral reefs growing in warm inland seas 400 million years ago.

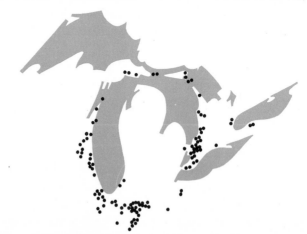

Deposits of pure rock salt, crystallized from the ancient seas when they evaporated, often lie buried on coral reef margins.

Dead Sea. Their salt content became so concentrated that it precipitated from solution, and year after year, century after century, the salt shimmered up through the water. With time, the salt beds and associated muds killed and buried the reefs. Under the State of Michigan the total average depth of salt, if it were compacted into one layer, would be one thousand feet. The beds of pure rock-salt found in the Windsor and Detroit area are up to a hundred feet thick, hidden under the shales and sandstones of the Devonian period, that later covered them.

When the seas were gone completely, layers of rock that had been sea bottoms throughout geological time covered the old Precambrian surface. In the Michigan basin, the layers of rock lay to a depth of nearly three miles in an enormous saucer of land two hundred miles across. Two hundred and fifty million years ago, the Great Lakes region had turned into a flat, monotonous plain, covering thousands of square miles. The sound of the surf and the lapping of the tides were gone. For many millions of years, there was just the sound of the streams that ran across its surface. Where these streams went, nobody knows. The continent was heaving and subsiding slightly; the layers of sedimentary rock eventually lay tilted toward the south, with the surface water and wind working on the edges of the layers. A wanderer over those desolate slopes, heading north across the edges of layers planed off by tens of millions of years of erosion, would have walked over successive formations of rocks, from the youngest to the oldest of the eastern part of the continent (and still would, if all the accumulations of soil were removed and he walked, say, from Fort Erie to Niagara-on-the-Lake).

Rivers etched the land into patterns, eroding the soft, sandy rock first and undermining the later layers of harder, more resistant, limestone. Great chunks of land collapsed from time to time, and slid down an eroded face of rock in a cloud of dust and debris with a rumble that shook the land. Ground waters ran between layers, dribbled down the cliffs and dissolved minerals from the rock. Rivers ran along the faces of the cliffs and other rivers ran into them, some cutting through the cliffs, making notches that grew wider through the ages. The result of this action – the undermining of cliffs that had formed along the edge of sloping layers of rock – produced ridges of land, smooth and sloping on the west and south, jagged and exposing

THE NIAGARA GORGE

At the Whirlpool Rapids, where the mighty Niagara cut through bedrock approximately five thousand years ago, the river has exposed two hundred million years of geological history. Scattered boulders line the swirling currents at the edge of talus slopes eroded from the sheer face of rock. The resistance to weathering of the hard dolomitic cap-rock is reflected in the upper ledge. Marine sediments – limestone, shale and sandstone – fill pages in the record of river deltas.

This waterfall at Jordan, exposing layers of shale, is an example of waterways that have etched notches into the Niagara Escarpment.

the strata of rocks on the east and north. As erosion continued, these ridges over millions of years wandered and drifted toward the southwest, as the rivers undercut them and their tops tumbled into the streams.

The forming of cuestas was part of this process, the most important of these, in the Great Lakes region, being the Niagara Escarpment. Its formation is due to the hard rim-rock – Lockport dolomite – resting on a bed of softer layers of dolomite, shale and sandstone. Like many geological events, cuesta-building was a slow process. At Dundas Creek, near the city of Hamilton, every time a chunk of rock slides down the cliff face, it is the latest, tiny episode in a story that reaches back to the dim beginnings of the land. The result can be seen at Webster's Falls, above the town of Dundas, Ontario. There a jumble of rock lies at the base of the cliff's face where it has fallen. Dundas Valley is one of the great notches worn in the escarpment by streams, Beaver Valley another. These are old valleys, cut a few million years ago, relatively recently by geological reckoning, but long before the streams we know began to trickle over the countryside.

During the period when the sedimentary rocks were being etched by erosion, the Great Lakes basin began to form. The deep layers of rock that had been deposited over what is now the State of Michigan were eroded in a way which created the Lake Michigan and Lake Huron basins. They were hollowed out from soft shales of the Devonian period, exposed at the edge of the former sea basin. The zone of relatively hard rock, in particular the rim-rock of the Niagara Escarpment and that separating the basin of Georgian Bay from Lake Huron, also cleaves the inlet at Green Bay from Lake Michigan. Lakes Erie and Ontario were hollowed out of the same sequence of hard and soft rocks. Lake Superior basin is the only one not laid down by the seas discussed in this chapter. This trough consists of much more ancient sediments and lavas belonging to the shield, dating back to Precambrian times. The depression is also much older than the basins of the other lakes – there may even have been a lake in this basin in very early geological times. The deepening and shaping of the Great Lakes basins, as we know them today, belongs to an altogether different and more recent sequence of events, that was to change the entire face of the land.

6 GLACIERS SMOTHER THE LAND

A million years ago a drastic change of environment took place. Nobody knows why, but gradually the temperature all over the earth had become a few degrees cooler. Ice caps on highlands in the northeast part of North America began to accumulate more snow in winter than they lost in summer. The ice began to build. It thickened and spilled down the valleys, fanned out on lower ground and formed small ice fields known as piedmont glaciers. These began to increase snowfall by chilling the air above them, and the new snow speeded the growth of the glaciers until they started to flow under their own weight. They buried the highlands that had spawned them, and merged to form a great continental ice sheet which began to move south. With every advance the glaciers altered the landscape, moulding the surface into new shapes under the tremendous pressure exerted by the ice.

At this time, the Great Lakes region was no longer the bald land it had been when the seas withdrew from the continent. There had been enormous evolutionary changes in plant and animal life. Marine plants and animals had invaded the land, and over millions of years adapted themselves to the new environment. Throughout much of this period the climate in the Great Lakes region had been tropical. Now the climate be-

came arctic. Caribou roamed wastes of tundra in what is now southern Ontario. South of the tundra were spruce forests, the sequence of zones being much as it would be if we moved all today's forest zones a thousand miles south. A high, glistening white expanse of ice loomed to the north.

This was the fourth time ice had invaded the region during what we usually call the "ice age." The first advance took place probably less than a million years ago. Between the four advances of the glaciers, there were long warm periods when the ice receded far into the north. Of the four major advances, the only one that very much is known about is the latest one, called in North America the Wisconsin. The glacier inched its way further and further south. Beneath its giant paws, trees were flattened like straws and dragged in the direction of the ice flow. In places forests of spruce, pine and birch were levelled. The earth's crust was depressed by the tremendous pressure, and the earth's surface sagged beneath ice that was a mile thick in the Great Lakes region. The Niagara Escarpment was a mere insignificant ripple beneath it. Winds poured down over the slopes of ice and above them was a blinding white world like the inside of a cloud. The advancing snout of the glacier was a desolation of sand and gravel scraped from the earth's surface and rocks rafted down from where the glacier had gouged them off the old land to the north.

Rocks were embedded in the bottom of the glacier like grains of sand in the sole of a shoe, and acted as a first-rate

Today the meltwater from a dying remnant of the Wisconsin glacier high in the Arctic forms a moraine of till (foreground).

grinding tool. Deep grooves were cut into the surface of rockfaces and hard outcrops, as on the Bruce Peninsula, and they were moulded into smooth round contours. The glacier widened the notches already cut into the Niagara Escarpment, reamed out the Beaver, the Dundas and other valleys and deepened parts of the Great Lakes basins. It smeared a blanket of clay and boulders over the land. It carried a rubble of rock debris to its margins, pried rocks out of the valley walls and carried the material along with it. There is no accepted explanation for the drop in temperatures that brought the glacier, nor for the general rise in temperatures that eventually stopped its advance.

The glacier began to thaw and rot away at its southern margin. Glacial streams flowed from great caves and mile-long tunnels at the base of the ice. Water poured down through the glacier in hidden waterfalls. The retreating snout of the glacier was a gigantic muddy mess of piled-up rock fragments. Sand was carried down by streams into fissures, to pile up and dry and blow around in the wind. Ridges of land began to show through the top of the ice and streams rushed down between these and the shrinking ice cap. The ice was still flowing, but melting just as fast at its front end. A zone of ice within the glacier acted like a conveyor belt, carrying the ice, rocks and mud that the glacier had picked up to the margin of the ice sheet and dumping this cargo there. The glacier left a mountain of rubble when it melted back, and between the ice and this end moraine the melting water began to form small lakes.

It was one of these pools that became the first of the Great Lakes, a patch of meltwater at the west end of the Erie basin, now known to geologists as Lake Maumee. It overflowed through the end moraines and drained down the Wabash River to the Mississippi. At about this same period in Great Lakes history, a shield-shaped trough, Lake Chicago, had appeared in the same way along the front of the ice that lay in the Michigan basin and drained down the Illinois.

The retreat of the ice wasn't an uninterrupted process. It made minor comebacks and the ponded waters underwent a continuous sequence of changes as the ice margins oscillated through the centuries. Some of the early lakes, during a re-advance of the ice, became so narrow that they must have looked more like deep blue rivers, the ice on the north shore

How ice shaped the land – just north of Toronto, the moraines of the 100-mile-long Oak Ridges roll across Albion Township.

towering above them like a white mountain. Imperceptibly, century after century, the lake would widen and the ice retreat further to the north, until it disappeared over the horizon. For hundreds of years the lake would look very much like one of the Great Lakes today. Then, in the north there would appear a faint white streak, barely distinguishable from a low white cloud, but growing sharper and clearer century by century, as it drew closer. The lake level would begin to rise, covering the old beaches, killing the plants that had re-established themselves in the region after the last ice retreat, rotting the roots of trees and rising up their trunks. The face of the ice would loom higher. The crescent of water would be there again, flowing down the end moraines until the glacier bulldozed its way through and effaced the gravel deposits it had left there earlier. The lake which had been there for perhaps a thousand years, would be gone. The region would again be an arctic world.

Something much like this happened to Lake Maumee, and it happened to Lake Chicago at the south tip of the Michigan basin, and to Lake Duluth, which had formed at the western tip of the Superior basin. Each time the ice withdrew, it exposed new territory and new, lower outlets; when it advanced, it blocked them again so that the outlets operated like a series of spigots at different levels, controlling the depth of the lakes. Early in Great Lakes history, a readvance of the ice pinched Lake Maumee to a small triangular patch of water a quarter its original size. Then the ice receded far enough north to expose a lower outlet. The water coursed along the ice face across what is now the State of Michigan to the Grand River valley and into early Lake Chicago. The level of Lake Maumee dropped forty feet. Another advance of the ice blocked this channel, and the level of Lake Maumee went up again by twenty feet and once more began to flow down its original outlet to the Wabash. Another retreat brought the level down eighty feet and the lake became a much larger one that now spread into a great bay around the present Saginaw Bay and cut a new, lower channel into the Grand River.

The ice was still receding. The arch of land in southwestern Ontario became an exposed island that extended west from the Hamilton escarpment almost to Lake Huron, and north from the area near London to Owen Sound. This exposed area, Ontario Island, was hemmed in by two lobes of the glacier. As the lobes receded, they left behind an interlobate pattern of debris known as horseshoe moraines with Mount Forest as their focus. Rivers of meltwater from the glacier poured between the ice and this island of ice-free land. Streams piled sand and gravel and clays on the bedrock, or the muds that the glacier had plastered over the land, building up the hills seen today in the district around Orangeville. As the ice wasted away, its margin divided into separate lobes which advanced and retreated independently, one lobe often effacing the deposits left by the other.

When the ice finally rotted away on both sides, it left a ridge a hundred miles long and up to eight miles wide from the Niagara escarpment around Orangeville to Trenton. This is the rolling land of the Oak Ridges that appears north of Lake Ontario. The thickness of the ice even at this stage was enormous; the top of today's Oak Ridges, now high above the surrounding terrain, was the bottom of a crack between two walls of ice. The burden of gravel and sand and clays and rocks picked up by the glacier as it scoured the ground and pried at the land during its invasion, was now dumped on the land, washed from the ice in streams of meltwater and plastered over the surface beneath the ice. Sand and gravel filled long tunnels that ran through the ice, and left behind the winding mounds of sand and gravel that lie today across the farmlands of southern Ontario. These welts on the face of the land are called eskers; one particularly high, long esker can be seen at the town of Norwood on Highway 7 east of Peterborough, Ontario. Highway 37 south of Tweed cuts through another such feature and a sign leading to a gravel path says "Esker Road."

The ice also dropped enormous boulders that it had brought down from the north, sometimes from a hundred miles away. One of these, a boulder of limestone that rises twenty-five feet above the ground, can be seen in a pasture west of Glen Miller on Highway 33, near lock No. 3 on the Trent Canal.

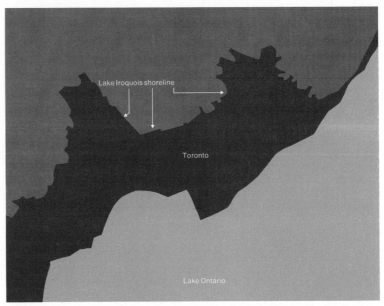

The shoreline of ancient Lake Iroquois, 180 feet above the level of Lake Ontario, would have run through the centre of busy Toronto.

The Glen Miller boulder – an "erratic" abandoned by the ice near the Trent Canal – is one of many rocks carried down from the North.

7 THE SHAPING OF THE GREAT LAKES

The Great Lakes were forming and reforming during the glacial epoch from the streams that came down off the ice. The story of the many phases of the Great Lakes is still being pieced together by geological detective work, from the location of old beaches, the depth of ancient channels, the calculated rate of down-cutting through spillways. Conflicting theories sometimes hinge on such fine points as whether, at a certain stage, the water flowed north or south from one lake to another. Certainly during one of the main, long stages, the region of Niagara Falls would have been strange and unrecognizable to us.

There was no Lake Ontario, and no Niagara Gorge. Ice lay over the entire area. The face of the glacier extended east and west from the region where tourists view the Falls today. South of it lay Lake Warren, a vast, icy lake that reached an arm to the east almost as far as Syracuse, New York, covered all the Niagara Peninsula, all southwest Ontario west of London, completely submerged what is now the St. Clair-Detroit area, extended north into the Huron basin as far as Kincardine, Ontario, reached half-way across the State of Michigan and drained into Lake Chicago and down the Mississippi. The north margin of this huge cold lake was a wall of the ice sheet itself, from which icebergs plunged into the water to drift around in the wind. The southern margin of the lake lapped a land where forests and shrubs had taken root in the mounds of material left by the earlier southern thrust of the ice. The falls at Niagara were thousands of years in the future. The Niagara Escarpment, over which the falls pour today, was alternatively buried beneath the ice and beneath the water of the lake. Today the top of the escarpment at Queenston is about 500 feet above sea level. The surface of this early lake at one stage stood at 690 feet. Its later stages of development are known as Lake Grassmere and Lake Lundy; the glacier still filled the Lake Ontario basin. Ribbons of water drained east along the face of the ice down the Mohawk and Hudson valleys to the Atlantic.

To a visitor looking out from those frigid shores, the position of the ice and water would have seemed an everlasting arrangement. No movement of the glacier was visible except for the occasional thunderous crash of ice sliding from its face. Yet, century by century, the ice in the entire Ontario basin receded, and the strips of water that lay along its face were widened and spread north to fill the western end of the Ontario basin.

There came a time, perhaps 12,000 years ago, when the ice face drew back far enough to expose a new low channel to the Hudson Valley, located near the present site of Rome, New York. The waters in the western end of the Ontario basin began to drain through this new outlet. Year after year the

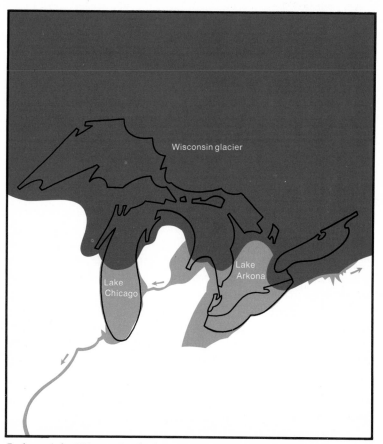

Lobes of the Wisconsin glacier were impinging on Lakes Chicago and Arkona 13,000 years ago. The main outlet for the overflow of melting ice was to the south. As the glacier receded, new spillways were exposed that caused the lakes to undergo numerous changes of shape and depth before they became recognizable as we know them.

level of the lake sank, until eventually the Niagara Escarpment was exposed. Lake Erie now drained over the top of the escarpment to a lower level. The lake at the lower level was the forerunner of Lake Ontario. At first the Erie waters drained to the lower lake by way of a small intermediate lake called Lake Tonawanda, which drained over the escarpment through several spillways. But gradually the drainage from Lake Erie to the ancestor of Lake Ontario concentrated in one main spillway that was to become the Niagara River.

The ancestor of Lake Ontario is called Lake Iroquois at this stage. Roughly the same shape, it was much higher and bigger than Lake Ontario, as it was blocked from the St. Lawrence Valley by ice that still lay in the vicinity of the Thousand Islands. The shoreline of this ancestral lake can be seen in many locations in Toronto. Yonge Street and Avenue Road climb its old beach. Davenport Road runs along the base of the beach, and the houses on the south side of Woodlawn Avenue are located on its crest. It must have been one of the most spectacular events in North American history when the glacier finally pulled away from the Thousand Islands. The waters of Lake Iroquois began to rush through this newly opened channel and eventually drained into the Atlantic.

Meanwhile the lakes in the Huron and Chicago basins joined in the great horseshoe of water, Lake Algonquin, which extended four hundred and thirty miles east and west, the distance from Lake Simcoe to Green Bay, Wisconsin. The ice was now in full retreat, and as it crept further north, it exposed lower outlets. Lake Algonquin started to discharge through what is now the Trent Valley system into Lake Iroquois. As the ice pulled even further north, the waters in Georgian Bay extended to where Lake Nipissing now lies, and ran along the face of the ice front to the Ottawa Valley and down to the Champlain Sea. This was the last stand of the ice in the Great Lakes region. There was ice around Lake Nipissing about 10,000 years ago, the last outpost of an unparalleled force that had invaded the land four times over a million years, and may yet return.

Lake levels have been subject to immense variations. Lake Ontario at one time was about two-thirds its present size. Recent research suggests that it may have been possible to walk between the tips of the Bruce Peninsula and Manitoulin Island about ten thousand years ago. This was at the lowest level of Lake Stanley, an ancestor of Lake Huron that stood at 350 feet below the present level.

The earth's crust around the Great Lakes, relieved of the tremendous weight of the ice, began to spring back to its present position. This uplift is still going on. At Root River, six miles north of Sault St. Marie, Ontario, the beach left by Lake Algonquin has risen over 600 feet. Over the last century the city of Kingston has risen in relation to Toronto at the rate of about eight inches every hundred years, and Michipicoten is rising with respect to Windsor at the rate of about twenty inches per century.

The bottom sediments of the ancestral lakes, into which the streams from the glaciers and the newly exposed land drained, form the lake plains of the Great Lakes region today. All southwestern Ontario is an old lake plain. The melting ice left other small lakes throughout the region. Lake Simcoe is the biggest of them. Bond Lake, just north of Toronto, was left by a single, isolated block of melting ice.

As late as the mid-1800s, geological events were often dated according to interpretations of the Bible. But when geology began to be taken into account post-glacial events were to a great extent dated according to the rate of erosion of the Niagara Gorge. But this in itself turned out to be not as clear-cut a process as was at first believed. The age given for Niagara Falls varied from 7,000 to 100,000 years. In 1841 Charles Lyell, a great British geologist and the first man to point out that Niagara Gorge had been created by Niagara Falls, estimated that the erosion might have required 35,000 years. But all estimates of the rate of erosion of Niagara Gorge were greatly revised by the technique of carbon-14 dating, a technique whereby the age of organic material, such as wood or peat moss, can be established by the rate of radioactive disintegration of one type of its carbon atoms. It is now known that Niagara Falls began to erode the gorge about 12,000 years ago. It took the glacier about 2,500 years to recede from this region to the area of Lake Nipissing. When it withdrew north of Lake Nipissing it ceased to have any influence on the outlets and levels of the lakes.

Opposite: This aerial photograph reveals earlier shorelines of Lake Nipissing (now Georgian Bay) resulting from changes in lake level.

8 THE FATE OF THE LAKES

A lake's destiny is to destroy itself. It grows wider and shallower. It fills up with sediment. Its beaches smooth out and the materials from them, eroded by wave action, settle to the lake bottom. Deltas build out from its rivers. The lake eats at its own shoreline, reaching further and further inland, and becomes shallower as it spreads. The lake is a catch basin for everything washed from the land, and everything that lives and dies in the water.

Waves along shores of the Great Lakes can be as big as those along many sea coasts. They reach fifteen feet in a storm, and ship's captains have reported waves twenty-five feet high in Lake Superior. Waves of this size can move tons of material in a single storm. Just as the waves of the sea do their maximum work during high tides, the lake waves do most of their work during periods of high water levels. Although the lakes have very little true tide caused by the pull of the moon and the sun, (it's around an inch and a quarter at its maximum) they sway back and forth in their basins under wind and differences in barometric pressure to create a sloshing effect called a seiche. Lake Erie will rise eight feet at one end and drop eight feet at the other within fourteen hours. Winds can cause sudden, destructive changes in lake levels. On June 26, 1954, a squall with winds up to 60 miles an hour drove in on Lake Michigan from the northwest and piled up an eight-foot wave that hit Michigan City, Indiana, on the east shore, about 8:10 in the morning. The wave rebounded and arrived at Chicago at 9:30 a.m., a formidable crest of water 10 feet high. At least seven lives were lost when the wave struck the shore.

The fluctuations of lake levels have been recorded over the last hundred years. The greatest variation occurred in Lake Ontario, well over six feet between 1934 and 1952, according to Canadian Hydrographic Service tables. Fluctuations in the level of Lake Superior may take as long as five years to reach Lake Ontario. When storms coincide with high water periods the waves cut into sand banks, undermine the roots of the trees and topple them onto the beaches; they chew away at the bases of cliffs until they are undermined and slump into the water.

A spectacular example takes place periodically at the cliffs west of Scarborough Bluffs in the Birchcliff area of Toronto. The cliffs here, although wooded, are receding at a rate of six feet a year. They're made up of layers of clays and sands. During a storm the waves hit them with a force that sends spray fifty feet up the cliffs. They scoop out the supporting material at the bottom, and the cliff, which has a definite angle of repose, slews off great chunks of land leaving notches at the top. This is a continual onslaught and there have been arduous and costly efforts to halt it, with temporary victories, but overall defeat. During a three-year period between 1957 and 1960 the cliff was built out with three thousand loads of fill until the dump trucks were able to drive out over the new land, but one day, just after a truck had driven back from delivering a load, the whole new cliff disappeared into the lake. One man who owns a house right on the cliffs has tried to anchor the land with cement blocks and twenty-eight-foot war-surplus barges that he had towed to the shore and sunk with sand. He had old car bodies dumped over the cliff, laced them together with steel cable and filled them with rocks. But nothing stood up against the force of the waves for long. The lake waves shift anything weighing less than five tons. In winter the shore is encased in solid ice, and in the spring, when this ice breaks up, objects on the shore are enclosed within huge pans of ice, perhaps twenty feet wide. Even gentle swells on the lake will rock the ice pan back and forth with enough force to pry anything apart or loosen it from the bottom.

The attack of waves is the most spectacular cause of erosion, but it's not the only one or even the most effective. Everything drains into the lakes. Nothing will stop the surface and underground water from reaching them. The man who fought the cliffs at Birchcliff with concrete blocks, one night just after he had bought his house on the edge of the cliffs, was lying in bed listening to water gurgling, trying to figure out how he could hear the waves lapping the shore 180 feet below. But when he went out with a flashlight to investigate, he realized that his house was on the natural drainage route that surface water followed to reach the lake. The water had piled up eight inches deep behind the house, had found its way through the back door, through the bedroom and out the front door over the sundeck. Spring water that seeps out between

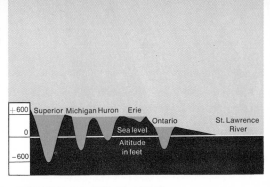

PROFILE OF THE LAKES

Lake Superior, the largest and deepest of the Great Lakes, has a surface area of 31,820 sq. miles and its maximum depth is more than 1,330 feet. Lake Huron is rivalled in its overall area by Lake Michigan. Shallow Lake Erie has the smallest volume. The combined discharge of the lakes is 234,500 cubic feet per second.

The Scarborough Bluffs, layers of glacial clay and sand, are eroded by waves.

Trees in sandbanks near Picton on Lake Ontario, demonstrate the force of wind.

layers of sand and boulder clay freezes in winter, and loosens the earth. In the spring the earth can be seen slumping down the cliffs and running out onto the beach like syrup.

One important effect of the glaciers was to disrupt the old draining system of the land. In this young system rivers are still wearing away the relatively soft unconsolidated clays and sands left by the glaciers and depositing them out in the lake basins. These are the catchbasins. Everything that's washed from the land and everything that dies in the lakes sinks to the bottom and adds to the thickness of the deposits there. A crop of hundreds of tons of tiny, often microscopic, forms of plant and animal life grouped under the general term plankton settle to the bottom annually. The rock materials weathered from the land are deposited in the lakes by rivers, then ground and sorted by wave action, which carries the finer, more buoyant materials out from shore. Great Lakes sands are relatively immature sediments that haven't been there long enough to be well rounded.

Far out from shore, below the deep water of the lakes, the material is fine clay. A core of this ooze, brought up by a small drilling rig or by a spring-trap device that clutches a sample of the bottom, consists of a fine, silky close-textured mud about the consistency of cold butter. It is sometimes banded in black and blue-grey or buff-grey, which turns to a uniform grey as soon as the iron sulphide of the black bands are exposed to the oxygen of the air. A core sample taken from Lake Michigan, which holds the complete cross-section of sediments, from glacial deposits to the present lake bottom, contained twenty-nine feet of

clay with grains averaging one and a half thousandths of a millimetre in diameter. Sediments at the bottom of Lake Erie, the oldest part of the lakes, are thirty feet deep in places and in some areas they are so thick they have never been penetrated by echo sounder. The lake with the least sediment is Lake Superior. It lies in the rocks of the shield where there's little soft material to erode. Skin divers report standing on barren subsurface rocks that remain uncovered by sediments after 10,000 years.

Sand dunes occur in the areas struck by western winds. Large amounts of sand have been deposited on the east shore of Lake Huron and near the Bay of Quinte at the eastern end of Lake Ontario. The origins of these sand dunes are in doubt, but it is possible that they were built up during the low water stages of the lake basins. All the more spectacular dunes on the Great Lakes are on the east shores where the prevailing westerlies have blown dry sand up from the beaches into ridges parallel to the shore. Perhaps the reason east winds do not similarly pile up dunes on the west sides is that they often bring rain that wets the sand and prevents it from blowing.

The most spectacular example of the constant change taking place on the lakes is the recession of Niagara Falls. The falls, when they first started to flow over the Niagara Escarpment, were located at the present site of Queenston. The top portion of the escarpment consists of hard limestone. Underlying this are relatively soft shales and sandstones. Century after century, the force of the water, helped by the loosening effects of frost, wore away the softer rocks until the hard capping limestones broke off and fell to the base of the falls, leaving a notch on the brink. Since this process began, the falls have receded seven miles upstream. The forces at work on the falls can be experienced at close quarters by taking a trip on the *Maid of the Mist,* a sightseeing ferry that bucks the water right up to the Horseshoe Falls. Five minutes after leaving the dock on a calm summer day, when the oilskins issued to the passengers seem a bit theatrical, the passengers are drenched by spray driven before a wind so strong that they have to shout into one another's hoods to be heard.

The distance the falls have receded from the site of Queenston would be an accurate gauge of how long the falls have been in existence, if all the factors were known – for example, the volume of water that flowed over the falls during the various stages of Great Lakes history, which would have an effect on the rate of erosion. Another important factor is the type of material the river had to cut through since its origin. This would seem to be obviously the material of the Niagara Escarpment which the river is cutting through today and which we can see exposed in the Niagara Gorge. But there remains the unsolved puzzle of the old St. Davids Channel. If you ride the whirlpool cable car out over the gorge, you can see that the cliff which curves around the whirlpool is not constructed like the cliffs of the gorge. There is no rock face. This cliff is a steep woody slope of a kind that might appear in any other part of the Great Lakes region. Geologists noticed this in the 1800s and in recent years began to drill down into the cliff to probe for the bedrock. They have found that this section of the gorge is the head of an old valley eroded through the bedrock and filled by soft earth materials. The glaciers apparently made a minor advance after the first Niagara Falls were formed, obliterated the falls and plugged this gorge with glacial deposits.

The discovery of the St. Davids Gorge would not in itself alter calculations about the rate of erosion of the present gorge, if they were two completely different channels. But the discovery of the St. Davids Channel led to the further finding that part of the present gorge is also an old channel filled by the glacier and re-excavated by the present Niagara River. The fact that the falls during part of their recession from Queenston may have cut through this relatively soft material has thrown out calculations based solely on rate of erosion. The best estimate for the age of Niagara Falls is 12,000 to 10,000 B.C., which means that the Niagara Gorge was excavated at an average rate of about three and a half feet a year since the river first began to spill over the escarpment.

If Niagara Falls continued to recede at their previous rate, without intervention by man, in about 20,000 years they would reach, and drain, Lake Erie (Lakes Huron and Superior would remain unaltered by this, as their levels would be maintained by the depths of their own outlets, the St. Mary's and St. Clair Rivers). But a counter force is at work. The land which is still springing back after its release from the weight of the glaciers, is constantly tilting the lake basins toward the southwest. The possible results of this tilting has been a fascinating subject for speculation since the Great Lakes were recognized as an aspect of glacial geology.

A commentary appears in New York State Museum's *Bulletin 45* by A. W. Grabau, a professor of geology at Rensselaer Polytechnic Institute in the early part of the century. He quotes from an article in a U.S. geological survey by G. K. Gilbert, who predicted that unless a dam was built to prevent it, Lake Michigan would again overflow to the Illinois River, "Evidently the first water to overflow will be that of some high stage of the lake and the discharge may at first be intermittent. Such high water discharge will occur in five hundred or six hundred years . . . after one thousand five hundred years, the Illinois River and the Niagara will carry equal portions of the surplus water of the Great Lakes. In two thousand five hundred years the discharge of the Niagara will be intermittent, failing at low stages of the lake, and in three thousand five hundred years there will be no Niagara. The basin of Lake Erie will then be tributary to Lake Huron, the current being reversed in the Detroit and St. Clair channels."

Contemporary geologists argue this point, however. One thing they know that wasn't known to Gilbert is that at Niagara the erosion is now under control and it can be virtually stopped. Hydro installations can now draw such tremendous quantities of water from the falls, that both the American and the Canadian cataracts can be reduced to a comparative trickle or shut off completely. In the not-too-distant future almost all of Niagara Falls could be dropped through pipes into power plants providing electricity for increased populations in the region.

WHERE CANADA BEGINS

Point Pelee, a spit of sand jutting out into the shallows of Lake Erie, forms the southern tip of the Canadian mainland. It is on the same latitude as sunny Rome and Ankara and thus boasts a flora and fauna that is unique in Canada. Buffeted by sudden storms and dangerous currents, the apex contains Point Pelee National Park, a nature preserve which attracts as many as seven hundred thousand visitors a year.

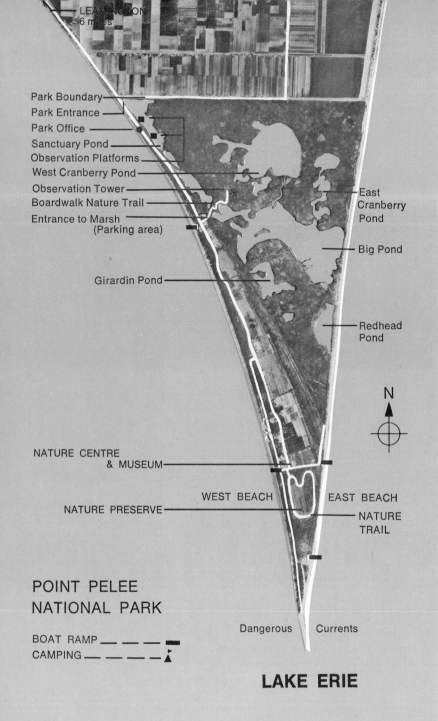

Park Boundary
Park Entrance
Park Office
Sanctuary Pond
Observation Platforms
West Cranberry Pond
Observation Tower
Boardwalk Nature Trail
Entrance to Marsh
(Parking area)

Girardin Pond

East
Cranberry
Pond

Big Pond

Redhead
Pond

N

NATURE CENTRE
& MUSEUM

WEST BEACH   EAST BEACH

NATURE PRESERVE

NATURE
TRAIL

POINT PELEE
NATIONAL PARK

BOAT RAMP — — —
CAMPING — — — —

Dangerous   Currents

LAKE ERIE

The changing shore

Point Pelee is part of a sandbank nine miles long and ten feet above lake level. Most of the birds, mammals and reptiles found in the region of the Great Lakes, and a few rarely seen anywhere else, exist here in almost primeval surroundings. Lake currents, storm waves and wind are constantly shaping and reshaping the unstable sands of Point Pelee. Gravel and sand are being deposited on the west shore while waves erode the eastern littoral, in places at the rate of two feet per year. Much of the vegetation tenaciously holds the sand in place, helping the fight against erosion. Without the protection of breakwaters, the peninsula would soon be divided by a number of lake channels.

Marshes bordered by woodland stretch to the eastern shore.

A small tree succumbs to the forces of wind and erosion during a storm on the west beach.

Nature attempts to hold the shifting ▶ sand in place by the progression of vegetation across the beach. The mature trees give way to thick grass, and finally to small plants growing tenaciously in the sand.

Spatterdock starting from a single plant can cover this pond.

Four square miles of marshland stretch to the horizon.

The nature trail winds through the lush forest growth.

A bonanza for botanists

The terrain of Point Pelee is mostly marsh or woodland. The major part of the park is a two-thousand-acre marsh, containing many large ponds. Here, water plants and sedges wage a constant battle with the open ponds, encroaching on them year by year, turning the area into a lush carpet of vegetation, including water-leaf and the rare swamp-mallow. Of the six hundred plant species found at Point Pelee, the greatest variety can be seen along the woodland nature trail, towards the southern spit of the park. It exemplifies the true deciduous forest, found only in this part of Canada. Hackberry and red cedar are abundant among the black walnut, red mulberry and white sassafras trees – festooned by exotic vines. Shrubs luxuriate in sheltered niches with hop-tree, spicebush and fragrant sumac contributing to flora rarely seen in Canada. Numerous distinct habitats are crowded into this relatively small area of 3,500 acres.

◀ *Along the edge of the pond muskrats find home-sites and a rich store of waterplant roots and stems to gnaw at.*

Opossums are marsupials, rearing their offsprings in a pouch.

The shy white-footed mouse (weight one ounce) is seldom seen.

A brush-wolf pup ventures out of its den into Pelee sunshine.

A perfect environment
for furry creatures

Animals found nowhere else in Canada enjoy Point Pelee's warmer climate. The eastern mole burrows its way through the sandy soil and the large rust-brown eastern fox-squirrel shares the shelter of the trees with the more common grey squirrel. Raccoons and mink are in their element among the marsh ponds, feeding on the multitude of creatures that thrives there. Muskrats build their community dwellings near the shore with under-water doors to guard against marauders. Other creatures of forest and pasture abound, including cottontails bobbing about among the brush and dense grass. A white-footed mouse may venture to the edge of the forest, where the graceful white-tailed deer browse among shrubs.

◄*A big brown bat roosts on the bark of a tree after a meal of flying insects; it can catch more than one thousand per hour, using its amazing supersonic echo-location sounds.*

Large flocks of waterfowl break the long journey up the Mississippi flyway to find a much-needed resting place.

The lesser yellowlegs stands
at the edge of a pond.

Cassin's sparrow,
an accidental visitor.

A saw-whet owl
guards its tree home.

The birds arrive

The pageant of bird migration during the spring is one of the great attractions of Point Pelee. From March to June warm air currents carry many rare birds northward across Lake Erie to alight on the tip of the peninsula, exhausted and in search of food. As many as 650 whistling swans and 20,000 white-throated sparrows have been counted in a day. In the middle of May, shortly after sunrise, more than 100 bird species join in the early-morning chorus, seldom equalled in eastern Canada. Black-crowned night herons and great blue herons can be seen on the wing. Visitors should start a tour at the sanctuary pond close to the entrance of the park where they'll observe dozens of waterfowl – joined by black terns – while rails and long-billed marsh wrens can be seen hugging the edge. On open ground nearer the woodland, look out for kingbirds and woodcocks, and up in the trees, cerulean warblers and redstarts. Piping plovers and spotted sandpipers prefer the sandy beaches. Offshore, egrets, loons and jaegers can be observed, while eagles hover aloft with the hawks whose migration south is a spectacle in late September.

A great blue heron returns from a fishing trip to the lake.

Wood duck (top) nests in hollow trees.
A red phalarope (bottom) rests on its flight north.

The black-billed cuckoo at its fragile nest with young.

This recently hatched night heron chick waits patiently for its food.

These bees in the centre of a trillium are necessary to pollinate the plant and this insures its reproduction.

An ant, cleaning its antenna on the tooth of a dead muskrat, will later help to carry away tiny bits from the dead animal.

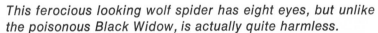
This ferocious looking wolf spider has eight eyes, but unlike the poisonous Black Widow, is actually quite harmless.

A green bottlefly sitting on the dandelion clearly shows grains of pollen caught in the hairs of its body.

Hurry, Scurry and Crawl

Some insects begin life in the pond feeding on frog-spawn only to emerge on the wing and be eaten, in turn, by the adult frogs and toads. These amphibians then make a tasty meal for the snakes and turtles of the region. The habits of many small animals can be observed in the varied surroundings of Point Pelee. The giant swallowtail butterfly and Fowler's toad are restricted to this part of Canada. During the fall, monarch butterflies, dragonflies, and wasps join the birds in their migration to the south, while spiders and other creatures that have outlived the summer brace themselves for winter survival.

The fragile beauty of much of the insect world is captured in this picture of a damselfly.

Wild-flower wilderness

One of the special attractions of the parkland is its variety of wild flowers. They make up a large part of the 600 species of plants growing here, and along the woodland nature trail many of them are labelled. Among the plants rarely seen in Canada are prickly-pear cactus, flowering spurge and swamp-mallow. Insect-devouring pitcher-plants grow in the wet locations, while hop-tree shrubs favour the beaches and act as host to the caterpillars of the giant swallow-tailed butterfly. For naturalists, Point Pelee National Park presents an unlimited field of study. The park is open all year.

Young off-shoots of prickly-pear cactus ▶ display their delicate blooms in summer.

Bloodroots blossom in the warmth of early spring.

Park ponds are garlanded by the rare swamp-mallow.

Clusters of seeds form on the hop-tree in June.

Cone flowers display their frail petals in spring.

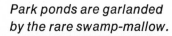

Rank-smelling skunk-cabbage thrives on moist woodfloor.

Carnivorous pitcher-plants trap the unwary insects.

Many-mouthed earth star is a rare variety of fungus.

High-bush cranberries nourish the Pelee winter population.

PART THREE / **PLANT LIFE**

AUTHOR'S NOTE: *In this and the following section of this book, plants and animals have been treated separately, but nature makes no such convenient division. All forms of life are interdependent. The little creature that lives on the lake bottom for two years before emerging as a mayfly for instance, comes under the heading "animals." But it would have no existence apart from its environment, the bottom of the lake, where it lies wafting water through an open-ended tunnel, straining out microscopic bits of plant life and stuffing them into its mouth like a baby eating pablum with two fists. A forest comes under the heading of "plants" but the deer that browse under its canopy are as vital a part of the forest's life processes as the soil and the rain. A deer spends most of its life like a living harvesting machine, steadily munching young trees, eating some and passing up others. The entire character of the forest depends on which young trees survive, and to describe the forest without the deer is to tell an artificial story.*

The plants and animals have been dealt with separately here, only for purposes of reference. Otherwise, one particular animal, say a grasshopper, would hop through the pages of this book much as he does in life, and to find out about him it would be necessary to chase him through paragraphs about sand dunes, lake margins, ploughed fields, bedrock and grasses, not to mention flocks of the birds that eat him. It is simpler to deal with grasshoppers under animals and grasses under plants, with the clear understanding that in nature these things exist together, one dependent on the other, as inseparable as the grass from the soil or the soil from the bedrock.

9 THE LAND BECOMES GREEN

Five hundred million years ago, all plant life – all life of any kind – existed only in the seas. A few seaweeds may have trailed some of their long tentacles up onto the land at the sea-margin, but they were essentially water plants, unable to survive on dry land. There was nothing resembling the green world such as we live in. Not a blade of grass or a shrub gave a touch of green. Rains came down on a naked land. Frost and wind and running water worked directly on unprotected rock.

What happened in the Great Lakes region during the momentous stage of evolution when plants made their first step onto the land, or during the hundreds of millions of years after, when the land gradually became clothed with plants and trees, is a blank page in the region's history. Two forces wiped out the record. It was a period of erosion in the area. Rocks formed from sediments that were deposited when this episode was taking place have been worn away from the entire region. Any lingering traces were scoured by the glaciers. Pre-glacial forests of some kind no doubt existed. South of the Great Lakes region, in Pennsylvania, Ohio and New York, there were luxuriant semi-tropical swamp forests that left the enormous coal deposits

of today. There were huge jointed plants like today's horsetails, a hundred feet high. There were giant ferns and trees with scaly bark like the skin of a reptile, trees with trunks that were bulb-shaped at the base, naked plants with stubby spines but no leaves. Green scum lay on the water, the forest floor was a spongy mass of decaying plant material, and through much of the period the atmosphere was steamy and semi-tropical.

When the record of the Great Lakes began again, the ice had come down over the land. Four times it levelled the forests, wiping out the record of life on land. It ground the rocks beneath it and turned the Great Lakes region into a lifeless, arctic land. But the forest always lay to the south where it had retreated, a forest by this time much like that of today. As the ice receded, the forest began to reclaim the land. First tundras and sedges gradually recolonized the areas left desolate by the ice, in the arctic zone close to the receding ice face. When the lakes were taking shape, these tundras and sedges probably crept over the mounds of sand and gravel left by the ice cap and grew up to the southern shores of the frigid lakes. As the ice moved north, spruce forests replaced the tundra. There were long inter-glacial stages, when the ice temporarily left the area and the weather warmed up with a climate four to five degrees warmer than it is today. The pawpaw tree, a sub-tropical tree with a fruit that looks like a stubby banana, which now appears only in the region bordering Lake Erie, grew north of Lake Ontario. Another tree that grew in this region was the osage orange, a tree today native to the region of Arkansas, with a fruit that looks like a green orange four or five inches in diameter.

One of the world's most important sites of inter-glacial deposits is the Toronto region, in the Don Valley and at Scarborough Bluffs. Arthur P. Coleman, who was for many years Dean of the Faculty of Arts at the University of Toronto, described these interglacial beds for the Ontario Department of Mines, in a report published in 1933. (Freshwater shells found on the banks of the Don, 30 feet above the level of Lake Ontario, had been described in the *Canadian Geological Survey* for 1863). "It was many years later, however, before the real importance of the finds of wood and shells along the Don was recognized, when, in about 1890, the city undertook to straighten the beautiful curves of the little river and to improve it by digging an ugly canal for a mile or two up the valley. In this useless operation, fine sections of the drift were opened up . . . Presently another bit of work provided opportunities for collecting, this time the levelling of the bottom of the valley, near the present Riverdale Zoo, for park purposes and to provide occupation for the prisoners in the neighbouring gaol."

When the Don Valley brickyard began operations, around the year 1886, even more important sections were exposed. At that time Government House overlooked the Don Valley. "It was perhaps not intended, when the Lieutenant-Governor's residence was placed where it is, that the representative of the King should have within sight beneath him the most interesting bit of geology in southern Ontario, but such is the case."

The bottom eighty feet of the Don quarry is the bedrock of Dundas shale laid down under seas that covered the region more than 400 million years ago. Above these shales are glacial-age deposits. (Coleman connected these with the advance of the ice that took place before the last Wisconsin advance, but it is now generally believed that they are early Wisconsin). In the lowest two or three feet of bluish grey boulder clay are blocks of granite and bits of shale transported by the glacier from the Thousand Island region at the east end of Lake Ontario. In the clay above this are slabs of wood and whole tree trunks, clam shells, some of them Mississippian forms not now found around Lake Ontario. The changes that took place between the laying down of the glacial boulder clay and the laying down of these warm climate muds must have been tremendous, but the two strata come together without any record of what happened in between.

This is a recurring puzzle in geology, two deposits that indicate extremely different conditions lying close together. The one in the Don Valley has still not been solved. The only definite fact is, that the muds were deposited over the glacial drift by a lake that was more than 200 feet deeper than Lake Ontario. It was earlier than the sequence of lakes described in Part Two of this book. Scarborough Bluffs are the eroded remains of a delta that was formed by a river much bigger than the Don, which flowed into this lake from the north "bringing down logs of wood from its undercut banks, leaves that fell in the autumn,

Tropical pawpaw (papaya) *trees with a rich yellow fruit range just north of Lake Erie.*

The spiny osage orange, once seen in the region, has since retreated to the south.

This maple leaf of an extinct variety was found in clay deposits of the Don Valley.

and sometimes carcasses of animals, which decayed and dropped bones or horns here and there on the muddy or sandy bottom. The wood is generally more or less decayed, and the logs are greatly flattened by the load of ice that burdened the region afterwards. In one of the layers of blue clay about half way up, great numbers of leaves were found by carefully splitting the thin sheets. Most of them were broken, but a number were perfect. The brown remains unless varnished with shellac curled up when dried."

Of the thirty-eight species of trees found in these deposits, three have not survived. Two are maple trees, named after Toronto and the geological name for the ice age, the Pleistocene: *Acer torontoniensis* and *Acer pleistocenicum*. The other is a honey locust named after the Don: *Gleditsia donensis*.

10 THE VIRGIN FORESTS

There is a romantic notion that before the Europeans arrived in North America, the forests existed in a state of natural perfection. They're called "primeval forests" or "virgin forests." But there never was a primeval forest in the sense of something in a condition of suspended animation. Trees died of fire, disease and old age. They were cut down by beavers and their roots drowned by beaver ponds, ravaged by storms, uprooted by winds and floods. They were crowded out by stronger trees and attacked by insects. Pines struck by lightning exploded as if they'd been hit by bombs, and anybody who has ever tossed a pine knot into a fireplace knows how efficiently a blazing pine faggot put the torch to the surrounding forest. There were burned-up areas from the first time man set eyes on North America. A natural forest is not a state of perfection, but a struggle for survival and a constant process of succession.

Nevertheless, what man did to the forests was worse than any destruction accomplished by nature. He was the most lethal invader of all. To the pioneer of this land, the forest was the enemy. He looked on it about the same way as a used car dealer looks at a lot of cars that he has to move to survive. Improved land was land cleared of trees. The forests were used for making potash, laths, carriages, barrels, furniture, fenceposts, gun

butts, firewood and log houses. Fences were made from the stumps of pines that grew eight to twelve feet in circumference and 170 feet high. There are people today who remember barns in southwestern Ontario floored with walnut. In their notes surveyors wrote sentences like: "The land here is good, but it's heavily timbered," the way we might write "the house is basically good, but badly in need of repair." An item in *Smith's Canada Gazeteer* of 1846 reported (of Scarborough township): "the land bordering the lake is mostly poor and the timber principally pine."

The Great Lakes region must have had an entirely different appearance. There probably are very few pines left standing as big as the trees cut in their thousands by the pioneers. The size of some of these trees can still be imagined by looking at the huge stumps in parts of Algonquin Park. Most of the big birch trees too, have disappeared. When in 1957 the National Museum in Ottawa commissioned an eighty-one-year-old Ontario Chippewa Indian named Matt Bernard to make a

Ganaraska Valley, virgin forest-land a century ago, was transformed into a grotesque desert due to severe erosion triggered by a forest fire.

birchbark freight canoe to preserve some evidence of this dying art, he travelled nearly a thousand miles in the Algonquin and Timagami regions to find birch trees big enough.

Before the human invasion forests covered the shores of Lake Ontario. In 1851 W. H. Smith wrote: "The orginal forest (Etobicoke) was predominantly hardwood and covered the whole watershed. The trees were large and widely spaced and rose to a height of fifty feet or more without a limb. The interior of the woods was dim and cool, with hardly any underbrush, but with a deep covering of duff over the forest floor. On the dry, level land, maple with its associate beech, and in some sections basswood, was predominant. On the wetter sites, silver maple, white elm forests with their associates of swamp white oak and shagbark hickory occurred, while on muck areas cedar grew in swamps and on the wettest sites, small areas of tamarack were found. A few acres of oak occurred here and there, but nothing like the extensive oak plains which were present on the Humber watershed, notably in the western part of

York township. White pine and hemlock grew on the well drained slopes and ridges along the stream valleys and occurred as scattered trees throughout the hardwood stands attaining their best growth in the maple beech woods."

There are no untouched patches of forests left in the Great Lakes region. One that has probably been least altered is Rondeau Provincial Park on Lake Erie. Pines were taken from here as from everywhere else in the Great Lakes area, but this is still a beautiful old southern-hardwood forest, a kind of forest that appears in Canada only in this southwest section of the Great Lakes region. The first thing you notice, about a mile south of the park entrance, is the height of the trees. The road goes through a deep green slot in the forest. Tulip trees, with leaves that look as if they had been cut off across the top, grow straight and black-trunked, a hundred and fifty feet high, with dark heavily ridged bark. These monumental pillars of trunks are forty inches in diameter, bare of branches near the ground. As soon as they are shaded by higher branches they drop off.

Young aspens provide construction material for beaver dams, while entangled trees, too difficult to move, yield their bark as food.

This beaver kit may grow to three feet in length. Its front teeth never stop growing, but they are constantly worn down by gnawing.

Often Virginia creeper gives the trunks of trees in the park a feathery look, from a distance. Wild grape vines drape from the trees and form great green shrouds above the forest floor. In some regions of the park young ironwood trees with straight horizontal branches give the forest a peculiar wavy appearance, as if seen from underwater. There are enormous white oaks, which in open areas of the park develop huge serpentine branches, and a blue beech which foresters claim can be identified in the dark by soft ridges beneath the bark that feel like muscles. The blue beech trees with their elephant-like grey bark grow in the sloughs. The swampy ground in these low places is jet black with the rotting and decaying matter of the forest and covered with maidenhair fern. There are big-leaved basswood trees with sucker branches growing low on the trunk, and shagbark hickory, a tree found only in the southern hardwood forests of this part of Canada, and chestnut oaks which just barely make an appearance in Canada in the region of Lake Erie and Lake St. Clair. Chestnut trees (not the horse-chestnut, which is an introduced tree) used to grow here, but about forty years ago they were attacked by a fungus disease which spread into North America from Asia and they have been almost wiped out on this continent.

Despite its inviting and romantic appearance, this is not an easy forest to move around in. It is thickly overgrown with tangled vines and roots and the mosquitos are murderous. Even the Indians did not move through them by choice; they followed worn trails whenever possible. But the hard work of getting deep into the woods is worthwhile. The forest is melodious with the sound of cicadas, spring peepers, and wood pewees. Northern (Baltimore) orioles flash against the dense green forest canopy. Bush fungus appears covered with brown spores as though it were dusted with cinnamon. A wood frog, a little brown jewel of a frog with a black mask, hops among the maidenhair fern that covers the forest floor. The place has a feeling of virgin forest, even though it has been raided for pine a few times during its history. A casual note to Colonel Simcoe refers to an order to take six hundred logs from ten to forty feet long from the point.

Rondeau is an example of a special strip of forest called Carolinian, that extends along the Erie and Ontario shore. It is the northern tip of the hardwood forests of the eastern United States. At the other extreme of the Great Lakes drainage basin, touching the north shore of Lake Superior, is a band of Boreal forest – the evergreen forest of spruce, balsam fir, tamarack and jack pine that covers most of Canada from Labrador to the Rockies and up to the sub-Arctic. Between these two zones – the southern Carolinian and the northern Boreal – lies the main type of forest for the region, the Great Lakes – St. Lawrence zone, which forms a link between the other two. This forest consists of a mixture of maple, birches, beeches and oaks, with pine, hemlock, cedar and other evergreens. There are few patches of this kind of wood left in the heavily cultivated lands of southern Ontario, and what examples there are have been ravaged by logging. The woods that come closest to their natural state are not necessarily in regions far from the cities. There are some dense patches of old woodland, in suburban Toronto, often amid expensive suburban homes, their fate depending on property values. You can see a small tract of this kind of woodland in the vicinity of Purpleville on the first north-south concession road west of Highway 400 on the Maple sideroad.

The land plants in the region of the Great Lakes have undergone changes not less radical than those of the forests. As the land was cleared for farming, the vegetation of the roadside and pasture became more characteristic of the region than the plants growing in the forest. Many of the common plants of the fields (and lanes, vacant lots and edges of unpaved parking lots in the city) are species introduced by the settlers. They are hardy plants that crossed the ocean in stores of grain and spread west and north from the eastern seaboard. Mullein, the fuzzy-leafed weed with a yellow flower that grows in rough pastures, is a native of Europe and Asia. Buttercups and chicory, the beautiful blue flower that comes out along the roadsides in August, are both native European plants. The common roadside thistle came from Europe. Yarrow, the flat-topped herb with a spicy scent that looks like a coarse Queen Anne's lace is a flower of Europe and Asia. Even timothy, the grass with the small green cat-tail top that's commonly used for fodder, is a foreign grass that was brought in by the settlers of southern Ontario; very fortunately, it turned out, as the native grasses of the Canadian forests would not have survived on lands that underwent such wholesale clearance.

11 HOW A FOREST IS REBORN

Even if the Great Lakes region had been left untouched by man, the forest at any given time would represent only a stage in a never-ending process. One of the best places to see the change and adaptation and succession taking place in a forest is at the south end of Algonquin Park. Highway 60 runs through grassy stretches covered with roadside flowers – orange hawkweed, fireweed, oxeye daisies, tufted vetch, beautiful blue viper's bugloss – but leading off from the highway, through massive gnarled, moss-covered rocks are hiking trails where descriptive accounts of the forest processes have been posted on the trees by park naturalists. Walking through the forest and reading these on-the-scene commentaries, you begin to get the feeling that a forest is not a thing, but an event. A yellow birch grows out of a white pine stump, the only spot not covered by maple leaves, which yellow birch saplings can't penetrate.

Young maples move in from all sides on an opening in the forest where the elements have left a jumble of dead trees beneath an open patch of sky. Carpenter ants are busy turning the fallen trees back into soil. Sphagnum moss grows out over an old lake capturing it for the land. Sphagnum is a pale green stringy plant that forms a spongy cushion as it encroaches on the lake. The entire covering rests on water. You can rip out handfuls of the moss and squeeze the water out of it, as if it were a soaked sponge. But spruce grows out onto this live matting while it is still so weak that the weight of a man on the sphagnum would make the top of a spruce twenty feet away bend over and wave, setting the entire surface of the bog in motion. (This is a very dangerous trick, as people have gone right through the sphagnum into the lake below.) Black spruce will grow on the bog, at first reaching a height of only three or four feet, but gradually bigger spruce will survive, and what was once a lake will eventually become forest.

Areas that were cleared of forests before Algonquin became a park, illustrate what must have happened continually in the primeval forests after fire had swept them. Usually everything burns up in a fire, although sometimes the fire sweeps so low, and moves so fast before the wind, that the tall trees do not

In a clearing where an old tree stood, honeysuckle and wintergreen spring up. They will give way to hemlock and a new tree succession.

Algonquin Park, covering an area of almost 3,000 square miles, offers a good illustration of the eternal cycle of forest life.

ignite. In either case the land is left blackened and barren of life, and a new forest begins to grow. Blueberries are among the first plants to return. When an emergency airfield was built just south of Mile 20 on Highway 60 at the south end of the park on a flat expanse of sandy land, deposited by an ancient glacial delta, the old pine stumps left by the lumbering operations of the 1890s were taken out or burned off together with all the brush that remained. Within a couple of weeks blueberries had covered the fields, along with sweet fern, bracken fern, sedges and grasses and several kinds of weedy plants that can grow under rough conditions. No bare land was visible.

The first tree to follow the low growth of this kind is usually speckled alder, and perhaps willow. Then come the poplar and white birch, which can grow in open sunlight and grow very fast. There's a beautiful little grove of these in the area of the logging exhibit at the east end of the park. Sugar maple can grow in open sunlight too, but the birch and poplar move in so fast that the maple doesn't get much space. Also the maples, al-though they can grow in open sunlight, prefer shade.

Once again, the forest begins to cover the area. There will be pure stands of poplar and pure stands of birch, and mixed stands of both. In the meantime, the soil has been enriched by animal remains and droppings and the decayed leaves and branches that have fallen from trees, and there is now a rich forest soil. But the birches, poplars, alders and willows are short-lived, perhaps reaching seventy-five years before they succumb to old age, disease or a storm. This type of tree is not tolerant to shade, and the young trees may not get enough sunlight. Seeds of other varieties of tree that do like shade are carried into the forest by the wind or animals, and begin to grow in the shade of the birch and poplar. These may be spruce and balsam, red and white pine, (and in sandy areas jack pine), red maple, and, later, yellow birch and beech, all of which tolerate shade, although in varying degrees.

Few maples appear in a small birch and poplar stand; the maples usually appear when conditions are more established,

SUGAR MAPLES
In a sugar bush at Athens, Ontario, the spring thaw swells a creek. The young trees growing in the vicinity may attain a height of 130 feet, in time, placing sugar maples among the tallest deciduous trees of eastern Canada. In autumn their leaves offer particularly bright colours. These trees yield the best maple syrup and the timber – from trunks up to five feet in diameter – is valued for its bird's-eye and curly grain.

but maples eventually take over the forest, because they can survive a denser degree of shade. Under this canopy of shade, largely sugar maple, a final struggle begins between maple and hemlock, the one tree under which maple cannot grow. But hemlock can grow under maple and under hemlock. Also, the seeds of most trees can't penetrate a deep carpet of maple leaves, but hemlock seeds can. Maple hold their own in the valleys, but hemlock takes over the dry ridges, although according to one theory this arrangement is only temporary. The maple stage, according to this theory, will last eight hundred years and end up with the hemlock winning and taking over completely. A hemlock forest is a sombre place of tall straight trunks, twelve to fourteen inches in diameter, bare of branches up to a height of twenty feet or more. The entire forest is shaded by the high branches, and the forest floor is a spongy carpet of needles. Sometimes a mere ten inches of soil covers the Precambrian rock. Outcrops can be seen, mottled with light blue-green and dark green mosses that cling to them tenaciously.

12 PLANTS THAT LIVE UNDER WATER

The plants that populated the sterile lakes left by the glaciers had long ago in the world's history adapted themselves to fresh-water life. Compared to the ocean, a fresh-water lake is a harsh environment to survive in. Fresh water is less buoyant. There is a danger to small organisms of being carried out to sea by currents. But fresh–water plants had been established for millions of years before the glaciers invaded the Great Lakes region. They existed in nearby streams and lakes to the south, ready to migrate to the lakes left by the glaciers. Sedimentation of the lake bottoms, erosion of the shores, solution of shore materials, the forming of ponds and marshes and beaches had gone on with the forming of the lakes, so that the general pattern of aquatic plant life that exists today was established very early.

A lake is a kind of frontier, settled, region after region, by invading colonies of plant life. This is an evolutionary invasion. Individual plants or generations of plants are confined to a particular environment, but their ancestors in the distant past

BLADDERWORT

This floating carnivorous plant can be traced above the water by a stalk supporting a yellow flower. Fronds extending from the submerged leaves are studded with bladders that trap and digest minute animals – one plant may contain up to 150,000 at a time.

DUCKWEED

The green blanket sometimes covering entire ponds is provided by duckweed, the smallest flowering plant. It does not have a true leaf or stem, but up to ten rootlets. The plants usually reproduce by the process of simple division. The name tells you they are a favourite food of many ducks.

WATER-WEED

Under favourable conditions, water-weed with its translucent leaves and fragile stems may choke whole streams. Its male and female flowers meet at the surface, but broken fragments of the plant will continue to grow. One plant may harbour numerous snails.

EEL-GRASS

The slender leaves of eel-grass, up to a yard long, extend to the surface and wave in the current, enfolding the spiral stem of the small green female flower. Male flowers float up to meet it. After pollination, the stem contracts with its fruit.

hundreds of millions of years ago, adapted themselves to aquatic life zones further and further out from shore. The common land plants of the forests and meadows live close to the water's edge in regions of moist ground, but they are still very much land plants, tied to the land by their structure and life processes. The shoreline of the Great Lakes is strung with some remarkably uniform pockets of plant life.

One specialized community that grows in wet sandy areas, usually former dunes, can be found from the top of the Bruce Peninsula to the east end of Lake Ontario: fringed gentian, a wet-meadow plant with a deep blue flower; grass of Parnassus, a bog plant with a white five-petalled flower; bladderwort, a delicate leafless plant with tiny yellow flowers; slender, erect orchids with white or cream-coloured flowers, occur in these areas. Communities of these plants can be seen at Dorcus Bay and Red Bay on the west side of the Bruce Peninsula, at Sauble Beach and Grand Bend on Lake Huron, at Pelee Point, Rondeau, Port Stanley and Long Point on Lake Erie. One of these sandy pockets can be seen on Toronto Islands at Lighthouse Pond, behind Gibraltar Lighthouse, and there are similar communities at Port Hope and Presqu'ile and Sand Banks Provincial Park in the Bay of Quinte area.

A colony that advances farther lakeward than the lakeside land plants is that of the marsh plants – the reeds and rushes that wade out into the water, but rarely advance to a depth more than three feet. The real conquerors of the water are the true water plants, not just living in water, but fully adapted to their aquatic environment. Some of these, like the floating water lilies and pond-weeds, with long flexible stems used like mooring cables, and leaves floating on the surface of the water originally invaded the land from the sea, but have gone back to the water. These plants, called secondary aquatics, have in their evolution coped with conditions more severe even than a lake, and for them fresh-water life is relatively easy.

Out from shore at a depth of nine or ten feet, a critical point is reached. Plants, if they are to survive in deeper water, have either to withdraw their roots from the bottom and float free, or go underwater. Duck weed is an example of plant life that floats on the surface. This is a free-floating plant with two small leaf-like structures from which a tiny root about a quarter of an inch long dangles into the water. But some plants have adapted themselves to a completely submerged existence on the lake bottom. Submerged plants cover the slope of a lake down to about twenty feet. The long green streamers that trail out from rocks and the underwater weeds that can be seen at the bottom of a clear lake belong to this group. Every type of underwater environment has its own form of plant life. Submerged rocks and sticks, viewed under a magnifying glass, become miniature forests of growth. But at depths greater than twenty feet plants run into difficulty because of the decreasing light, a situation that is overcome by the floating algae, the plant portion of the microscopic mass of life called plankton, which can exist in suspension far out in the lake, performing the processes of green plants in sunlight on land. The plant life of a lake is a rich and abundant form of life that, by and large, you don't see.

A glass of water dipped out of the lake looks clear, although it may bear a faintly yellowish tinge in a lake with an exceptionally prolific bloom, like the west end of Lake Erie. But, seen under a magnifying glass, it is a botanical (and zoological) garden, with its own crop of tiny floating plant life, spring, summer and autumn annuals, perennials and the tiny animals that feed on them, grouped generally under the name of plankton. In the Great Lakes there is an enormous crop of hundreds of tons of plankton annually. The plant plankton performs the same vital function in the food chain of the lakes that the green plants and grasses do on land, and all aquatic life ultimately depends on it. The plankton eaters are at the base of the pyramid of animal life in the lakes.

Plants are one of the factors that contribute to the ultimate destruction of a lake. They continually capture new water areas for the land. In marshes around the Great Lakes this takes place so rapidly that dry land will be created from some submerged areas within a couple of years. It can be seen happening at Point Pelee, where a big cattail marsh is protected from the waves of Lake Erie by tree-covered sand ridges. These ridges are permeable by water, and the level of the marsh varies with levels in Lake Erie. When the levels are down, shore-line plants invade the marsh: plants like jewel weed, nettles and some of the grasses. But the continuous and ultimately victorious invaders are the cattails. The roots of these plants float on the surface of the water, and when the plant dies the roots sink, building up the bottom of the marsh until it becomes dry land.

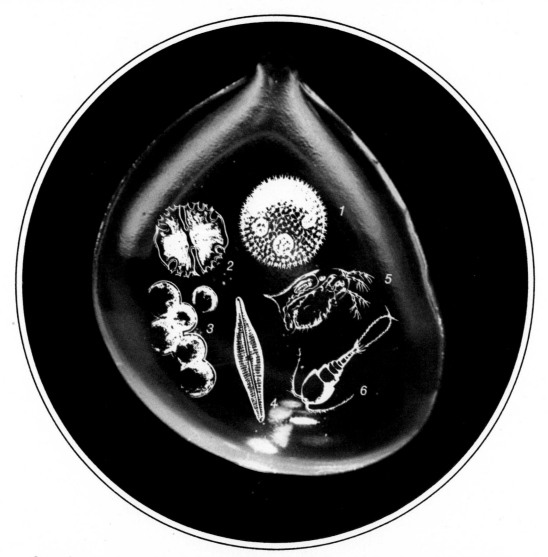

Superimposed on this greatly magnified photograph are drawings of microscopic organisms representing the pulsing life within a drop of fresh clear water. 1 Volvox alga, 2 Desmid alga, 3 Chlorella alga, 4 Diatom, 5 Daphnia with embryo, 6 Rotifer

THE FRESH-WATER WORLD

A multitude of life flourishes in the greatest expanse of fresh water on the globe – from microscopic plankton to lake sturgeon seven feet long – but nature's balance is endangered by man's criminal abuse of this priceless heritage. .

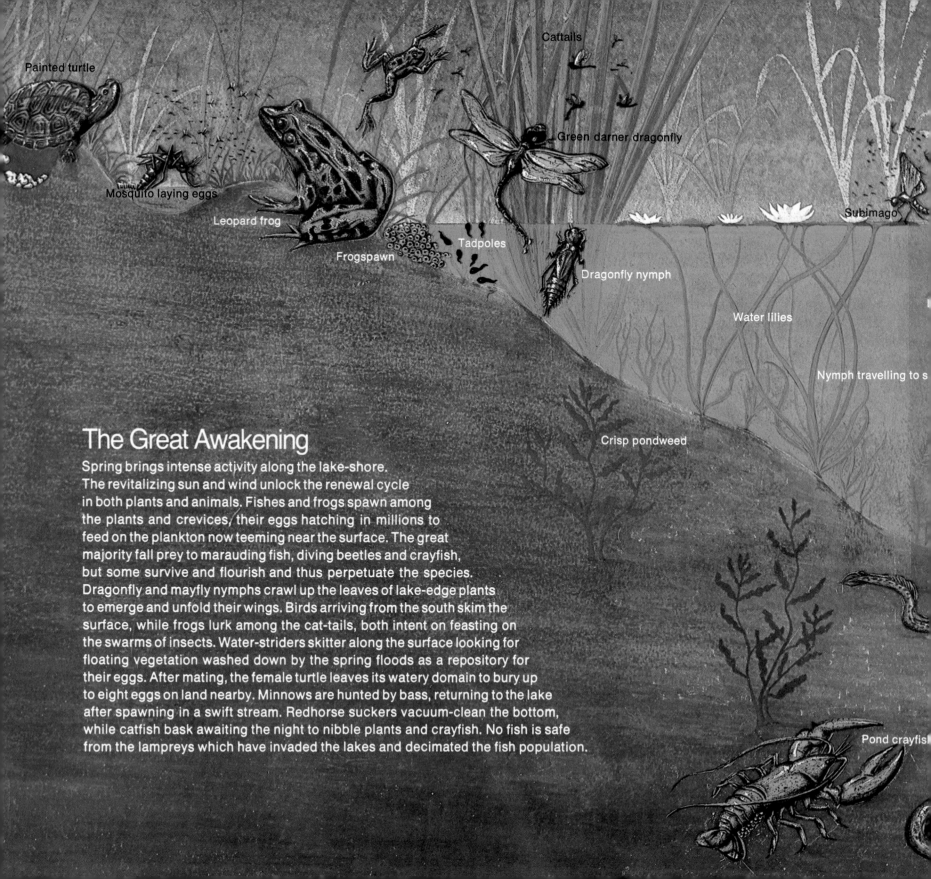

Painted turtle

Mosquito laying eggs

Cattails

Green darner dragonfly

Leopard frog

Frogspawn

Tadpoles

Subimago

Dragonfly nymph

Water lilies

Nymph travelling to s

Crisp pondweed

Pond crayfish

The Great Awakening

Spring brings intense activity along the lake-shore.
The revitalizing sun and wind unlock the renewal cycle
in both plants and animals. Fishes and frogs spawn among
the plants and crevices, their eggs hatching in millions to
feed on the plankton now teeming near the surface. The great
majority fall prey to marauding fish, diving beetles and crayfish,
but some survive and flourish and thus perpetuate the species.
Dragonfly and mayfly nymphs crawl up the leaves of lake-edge plants
to emerge and unfold their wings. Birds arriving from the south skim the
surface, while frogs lurk among the cat-tails, both intent on feasting on
the swarms of insects. Water-striders skitter along the surface looking for
floating vegetation washed down by the spring floods as a repository for
their eggs. After mating, the female turtle leaves its watery domain to bury up
to eight eggs on land nearby. Minnows are hunted by bass, returning to the lake
after spawning in a swift stream. Redhorse suckers vacuum-clean the bottom,
while catfish bask awaiting the night to nibble plants and crayfish. No fish is safe
from the lampreys which have invaded the lakes and decimated the fish population.

Bank swallow

Rough-winged swallow

Adult laying eggs

Shed skin

Water striders laying eggs

cycle of mayfly

Diving beetle

Male water-bug carrying eggs on back

Water flea (enlarged)

Green sunfish

Bluegill sunfish

Large-mouth bass

Eggs settling

Nymph on bottom

Sago pond-weed

Nymphs burrow in mud

Rock bass

Redhorse sucker

Pondweed

of large-mouth bass

Bullhead catfish

Blunt-nose minnows

Nest of rock-bass

Nest of catfish

Blunt-nose minnows' eggs under rock

amprey

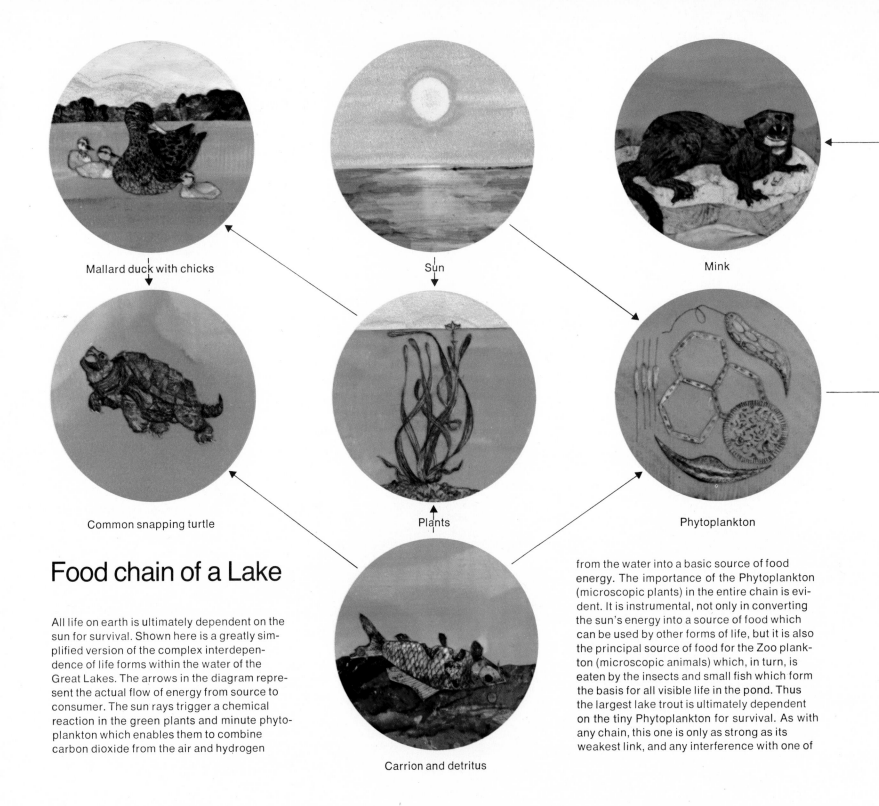

Mallard duck with chicks

Sun

Mink

Common snapping turtle

Plants

Phytoplankton

Food chain of a Lake

All life on earth is ultimately dependent on the sun for survival. Shown here is a greatly simplified version of the complex interdependence of life forms within the water of the Great Lakes. The arrows in the diagram represent the actual flow of energy from source to consumer. The sun rays trigger a chemical reaction in the green plants and minute phytoplankton which enables them to combine carbon dioxide from the air and hydrogen

Carrion and detritus

from the water into a basic source of food energy. The importance of the Phytoplankton (microscopic plants) in the entire chain is evident. It is instrumental, not only in converting the sun's energy into a source of food which can be used by other forms of life, but it is also the principal source of food for the Zoo plankton (microscopic animals) which, in turn, is eaten by the insects and small fish which form the basis for all visible life in the pond. Thus the largest lake trout is ultimately dependent on the tiny Phytoplankton for survival. As with any chain, this one is only as strong as its weakest link, and any interference with one of

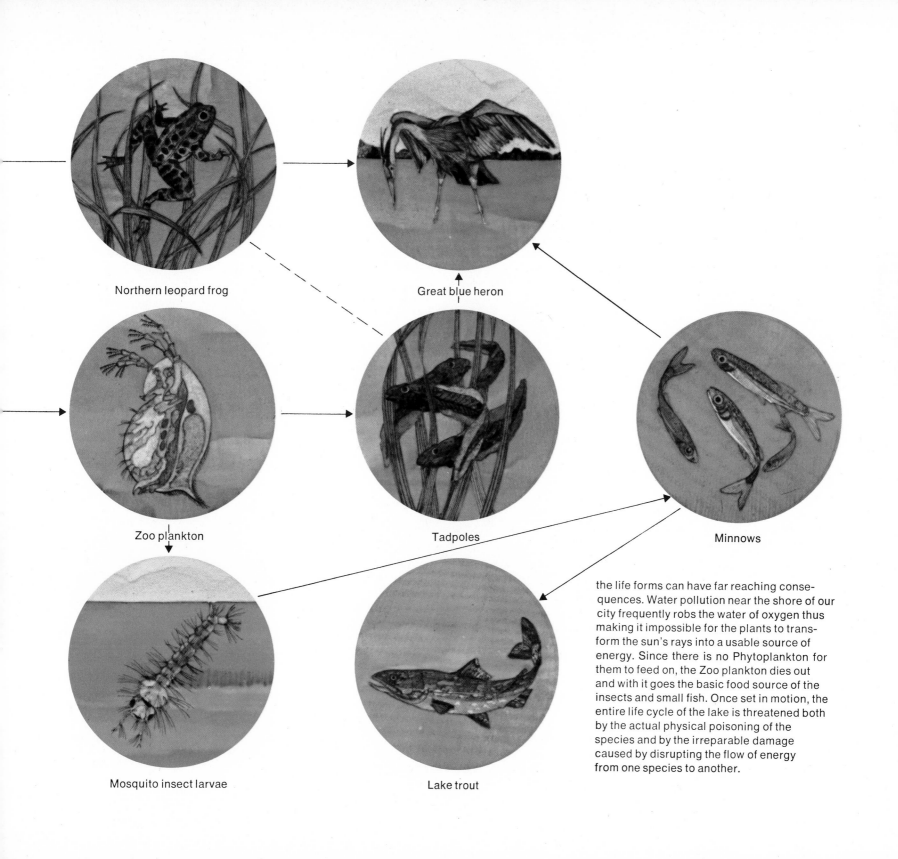

Northern leopard frog

Great blue heron

Zoo plankton

Tadpoles

Minnows

Mosquito insect larvae

Lake trout

the life forms can have far reaching conse-
quences. Water pollution near the shore of our
city frequently robs the water of oxygen thus
making it impossible for the plants to trans-
form the sun's rays into a usable source of
energy. Since there is no Phytoplankton for
them to feed on, the Zoo plankton dies out
and with it goes the basic food source of the
insects and small fish. Once set in motion, the
entire life cycle of the lake is threatened both
by the actual physical poisoning of the
species and by the irreparable damage
caused by disrupting the flow of energy
from one species to another.

The Layers of The Lakes

All life in the lakes lives in a clearly defined region, although they may range widely in search of food. The number of species of both plants and animals is directly related to the depth of the water. The shallows near the shore provide the warmest environment and also the richest oxygen content because the suns rays are able to penetrate all the way to the bottom and thus support a great deal of plant life. The Zoo plankton and Phytoplankton are found in abundance here, as are small fish, reptiles like the frog, snakes, etc., and a myriad of insects. This wealth of food causes the shoreline to be frequently visited by other fish in search of food. These fish, in turn, are eaten by the larger game fish which normally lurk in deeper water. As one gets deeper into the lake the amount of plant life decreases because of the lack of sunlight. This results in less oxygen being produced which means that fewer fish are able to survive here. The water temperature is directly affected both by the depth and by the season of the year. In winter all fish must move away from the shoreline to avoid being trapped in the ice.

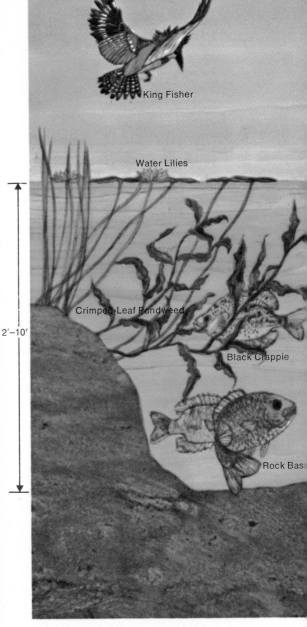

The first two feet of any lake, with its high oxygen content, is crowded with plant and animal life. The cattails and bull-rushes are among the most familiar water-plants while the minnows and tadpoles are frequently so common they can be caught with a fine mesh net and used for bait.

Small game fish are usually found in less than ten feet of water. Here they find sufficient plant life which can be used for cover and they are also close enough to the shore to be able to catch small fish and insects for food.

Canada Geese

15'

Pike

Wild Celery

Water Milfoil

50'

Lake Trout

Crayfish

Clams

200'

Tubifex worms

The larger game fish tend to prefer the cooler waters nearer the centre of the lake. The plant life here becomes restricted to those varieties which produce long stalks capable of traversing the distance between the lake bottom and the depth of penetration of the suns rays.

The lack of sunshine and the lower oxygen content as well as the colder water temperature, produces an environment suitable for few species. The lake trout is a frequenter of these depths and a few crayfish, clams and snails are also found here.

The only life which survives at these depths, the small tubifex worms, does so because of the yearly circulation of lake water. The water on the bottom, which is very poor in oxygen content, gradually rises to the surface during the spring and fall. The oxygen rich surface layer carries life-giving oxygen as it sinks to the bottom.

WINTER

PHOTOSYNTHESIS

SPRING AND FALL

Coldest layer

No circulation under ice

Energy from sun used
in photosynthesis

Oxygen produced by plants

Oxygen

Nutrients

Cold

Cold

Oxygen and nutrients
gradually used up

No light—no photosynthesis

Mineral and organic
matter circulates

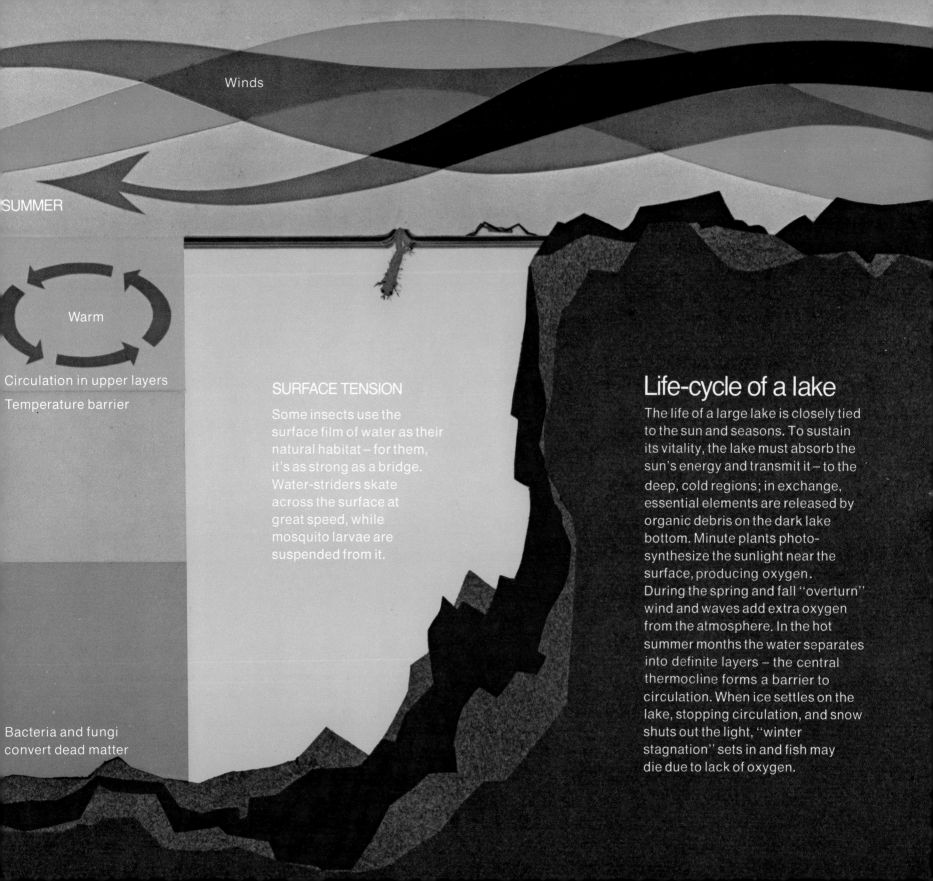

Winds

SUMMER

Warm

Circulation in upper layers

Temperature barrier

Bacteria and fungi
convert dead matter

SURFACE TENSION

Some insects use the
surface film of water as their
natural habitat – for them,
it's as strong as a bridge.
Water-striders skate
across the surface at
great speed, while
mosquito larvae are
suspended from it.

Life-cycle of a lake

The life of a large lake is closely tied
to the sun and seasons. To sustain
its vitality, the lake must absorb the
sun's energy and transmit it – to the
deep, cold regions; in exchange,
essential elements are released by
organic debris on the dark lake
bottom. Minute plants photo-
synthesize the sunlight near the
surface, producing oxygen.
During the spring and fall "overturn"
wind and waves add extra oxygen
from the atmosphere. In the hot
summer months the water separates
into definite layers – the central
thermocline forms a barrier to
circulation. When ice settles on the
lake, stopping circulation, and snow
shuts out the light, "winter
stagnation" sets in and fish may
die due to lack of oxygen.

1) Nest building

2) Egg-laying

3) Larvae in mud

The scourge of the lakes

The sea-lampreys invaded the Great Lakes through the Welland Canal in the early 1930s. Ascending swift-flowing lake tributaries, they lay their eggs in shallow depressions on rocky stream-beds. When the larvæ hatch

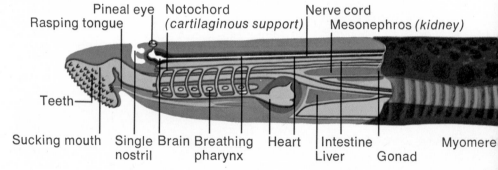

Rasping tongue · Pineal eye · Notochord *(cartilaginous support)* · Nerve cord · Mesonephros *(kidney)*

Teeth

Sucking mouth · Single nostril · Brain · Breathing pharynx · Heart · Intestine · Liver · Gonad · Myomere

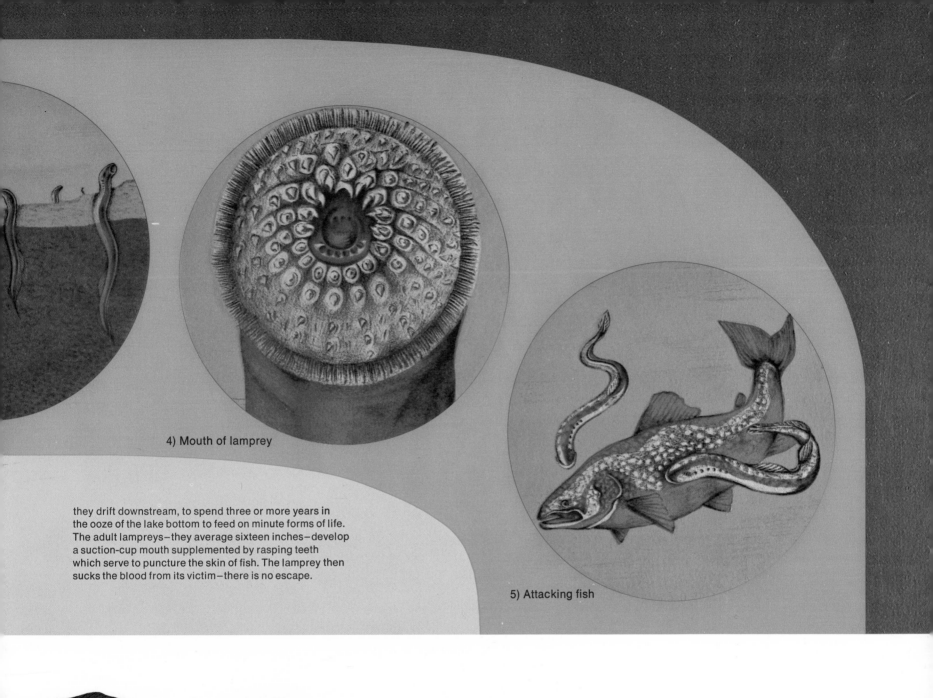

4) Mouth of lamprey

they drift downstream, to spend three or more years in the ooze of the lake bottom to feed on minute forms of life. The adult lampreys—they average sixteen inches—develop a suction-cup mouth supplemented by rasping teeth which serve to puncture the skin of fish. The lamprey then sucks the blood from its victim—there is no escape.

5) Attacking fish

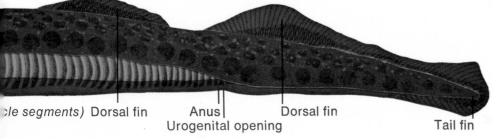

cle segments) Dorsal fin   Anus   Dorsal fin

Urogenital opening   Tail fin

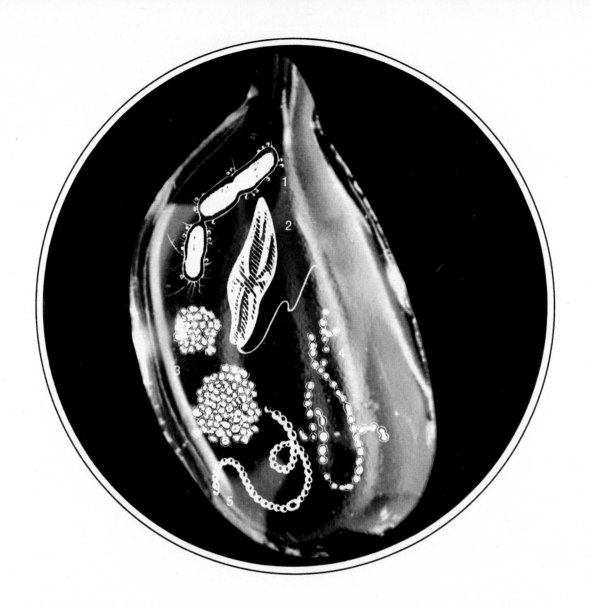

Life persists even under the most adverse conditions. With increasing pollution the Great
Lakes plankton is being replaced by new species of microscopic life – exceedingly prolific
but detrimental to most larger forms of life. And that most certainly includes man.
To represent a drop of polluted water, the artist has magnified algae and bacteria
that indicate the degree of contamination. (Compare with the illustration on page 81.)
1 Escherichia coli, 2 Euglina viridis, 3 Staphylococci, 4 Streptococci, 5 Blue-green algae.

PART FOUR / ANIMAL LIFE

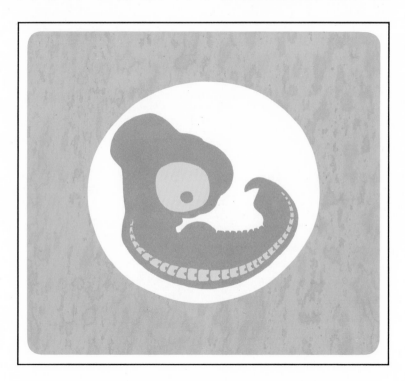

13 CROSSING THE BARRIER

The ancient seas that lay over the Great Lakes region swarmed with animals that lived in shells or in some other kind of hard protective covering. Their fossil remains,crystallized by chemical processes that turned them into stone, are found in rock formations throughout southern Ontario in enormous numbers. Quarrymen at the Toronto Brickyards work up to their ankles in the fossils of life that existed in the region hundreds of millions of years ago. These marine animals floated, swam and crawled over the ocean muds. Animals called crinoids, distant relative of the present day starfish lived anchored to the sea bed like flowers, gathering food with waving tentacles. Fragile colonies of little creatures called graptolites, a class of animal that had freed itself from the ocean floor, floated on the surface connected in colonies to form drifting masses, a kind of raft with tiny soft-bodied animals protruding from it.

Corals built their vast colonies that looked like sponges and honeycomb. Animals called cephalopods, ancient ancestors of modern squid and cuttlefish, with head and tentacles protruding from the wide end of a long cone, grew to four feet long. An animal called a trilobite, a creature something like a horseshoe crab, with a semi-circular headshield, became one of the most successful forms of life in those distant ages. Trilobites crawled or swam for short distances on the sea floor. Some species lay in burrows waiting for their prey to float by, some fed on the bottom muds, straining in nourishment from specks of plant life. There were trilobites that had eyes on top of their heads and they could roll themselves into hard pills to protect their bellies. At birth they looked something like tadpoles and grew by adding segments to their bodies. Trilobites developed into many species, reaching lengths up to eighteen inches, they dominated the seas for a long time.

Although the rocks of the Great Lakes region are among the richest fossil-bearing deposits in the world, there is a tremendous gap in the record following the time the continental seas withdrew, 300 million years ago. Before this time, scorpions had made the momentous step of adventuring onto land, probably living a marginal life at the side of the sea, but nevertheless establishing a beach-head. They were followed at a later stage by the amphibians, and later still, reptiles like the giant dinosaurs invaded the land.

To the south of the Great Lakes region, there are rocks bearing fossil remains and footprints of these great animals, and at one time there were rocks in the Great Lakes region that may have borne the same records. But the retreat of the seas from the Great Lakes area was followed by a period of erosion. The upper layers of rocks that may have carried the fossil remains of these animals were worn from the land by water, frost and wind over a period of millions of years. Later, within the past million years, the area was given a further scouring by the glaciers. So far, no trace has been found of the animals that existed around the Great Lakes during a period of 300 million years.

Even the record of life during the ice age is blurred and fragmentary until the withdrawal of the last of four glacial advances – the Wisconsin. From inter-glacial deposits in the Don Valley and at Scarborough Bluffs, something is known of a few animals that lived between the advances of the ice in the region of Toronto. Bones and ivory are found in bogs and clay and in the gravel beds laid down by the final waning of the ice lobes. The skull of a giant grizzly bear, unlike any existing today, was found in a load of gravel being shovelled into the basement of a new home being built in Orillia in 1964. The skull was turned over to the Royal Ontario Museum; zoologists reserved judgement until Carbon-14 dating definitely placed it at about 11,700 years old.

Giant beavers felled trees and built their dams in the ancient forests. There was a browsing animal, neither deer nor elk, but something in between. Elephants browsed on the twigs of evergreens in the bogs around the Great Lakes – not true elephants, but mastodons, shaggy elephants with coarse brown twisted hair two inches in length and long sloping heads. Their bones and enormous curved tusks have been dug up on farms and unearthed by bulldozers on excavation sites throughout southwestern Ontario. The remains of one mastodon was found during the digging of the foundation for Eaton's store in downtown Toronto, and many have been found in bogs along the shores of Lake Erie.

The mastodon lived in the evergreen forests around the

Great Lakes region for a million years. It may have evolved from mastodon-like animals that existed on the continent twenty-five million years ago, or it may have crossed from Asia over the land bridge that then spanned the Bering Strait. It was an animal of the bogs and spruce forests, yet for some reason, as the evergreen forests moved north with the retreat of the glaciers, the mastodons did not migrate with it. Perhaps it was because the evergreen forests were now up on the hard, rocky shield, an entirely different kind of land from the soft, fertile plains of the Great Lakes where herds of mastodon browsed in the bogs and came to drink on the shores of Lake Erie in the evenings. Perhaps it was because the mastodons were now cut off from the main evergreen forests by a kind of wood they found alien and inhospitable.

The land was becoming dry, streams were more clear-cut. As they drained the old lake plains, a new kind of forest of pine and oak and maples covered the land that was getting warmer and drier. Isolated, lone groups of mastodons were crashing through dwindling patches of the spruce bogs that once covered the region. The mastodon was trapped by a shrinking environment. The right kind of food was scarce and the few remaining animals were growing weaker and more susceptible to disease. Their number sank below the critical point, and about 6,000 years ago, the last mastodon died.

As the glaciers pulled back from the Great Lakes region, about 13,000 years ago, animals followed the slow northward retreat of the ice face. This may suggest herds of animals migrating north mile by mile, but nothing like this happened. Generations of animals were born, lived and died in the same territory, while the ice lay in virtually the same position for a hundred years or more, as if the world had always been arranged that way and always would be. But the ice was receding nevertheless, and over hundreds of generations whole species of animals extended their range further north. Perhaps an individual animal discovered the bank of a stream an eighth of a mile away that had become warm enough and was surrounded by the right kind of growth for its own particular way of life. Its descendants would adopt the spot as their permanent territory. Gradually, over tens of thousands of years, almost foot by foot, the range of a species extended.

But in the Great Lakes region, the lakes themselves formed an enormous barrier between animals the ice had driven south and the Canadian shore of the Lakes. Some animals returned around the west end of Lake Superior and some around the east end of Lake Ontario at the Thousand Islands. They crossed at the Sault and around either end of Lake Erie, at Niagara Falls or the St. Clair and Detroit Rivers. There were periods during the formation of the glacial lakes when there was dry land between the upper and lower lakes. There was a land bridge between Lake Algonquin and Lake Iroquois. But the animals also swam the rivers and crossed the ice in winter. Smaller forms of life probably crossed accidentally on driftwood. The Great Lakes are still a formidable barrier to birds. Even some big birds, like hawks, are not anxious to cross the open expanse of the lakes. But as the ice left the land to the north free, birds island-hopped across the lakes as they do today, to their new territory.

The result of these migrations was a wide dispersal of animal life. In some cases it created separate subspecies. Today there are two subspecies of moose in the eastern and western parts of Ontario. During the maximum extent of the Wisconsin glacier, the moose had been driven south to two areas in eastern North America that were separated by grasslands. Moose are animals of the evergreen forests and the grasslands kept the two groups apart. When the ice retreated, the animals to the west of the grassland came back into the Great Lakes region around Lake Superior. The ones east of the grassland came back by way of the Thousand Islands. The type found in western Ontario is the one of Michigan and Minnesota and west to British Columbia and the Yukon. The Eastern Moose, the form found in central northern Ontario is the one that appears in Maine, Nova Scotia and Quebec.

Even more pronounced separations occured in the smaller forms of life. The camel cricket, a little wingless humpbacked cricket with long feelers that lived under logs as well as in caves and the burrows of animals, got across at Niagara and the Thousand Islands. The eastern and western contingents wandered a long way, following separate paths of evolution. Today, on the north shore of the lake, there are three species that have one common ancestor far to the south of the lakes. There are regions north of the lakes that still haven't "filled in" with some species of wild life.

There is a gap in many forms of life north of Lake Ontario and Lake Erie. One of these is an antlion with gauzy black-mottled wings. It lays its eggs in a hole in a sand dune where the larvae live on ants that slip and fall in on top of them. This insect is found on the north shore of Lake Erie and at the east end of Lake Ontario, but doesn't appear in the space between. The same situation seems to exist with a moth called *Apatelodes angelica,* which is related to the silk moth. A heavy brownish-black beetle, called rhinoceros beetle, has spread along the north shore of Lake Erie, Lake Ontario west of Toronto and the region of the Thousand Islands, but hasn't been found anywhere in between.

While the early glacial lakes created a barrier to most forms of life, they changed the pattern of animal life in other ways as well. The old lakes were much bigger than the present ones and at one time there was a continuous strip of beach right through to the eastern shore. One of the inhabitants of this kind of terrain is a light-coloured grasshopper with black-margined yellow wings that almost disappears from view when it lands on sand. This grasshopper followed a strip of sand dunes that in early times were continuous to the Champlain Sea and the coast. Now it is found in sandy areas of the Atlantic coast and in isolated colonies on the north shore of the Great Lakes, where it has been cut off by the shrinking of the lakes. The Great Lakes form of this insect have by now evolved into a subspecies.

The most recent crossing of the Great Lakes barrier was made by a species of termite, which was first recorded north of the lakes in 1938. It crossed with the help of man, arriving in a shipment of sand delivered to a lumberyard in East Toronto for use in the manufacture of a cleaner. But some animals are still working their way around the lakes, as they did ten thousand years ago when the ice withdrew from the area. Since time immemorial bobcats have existed in southwestern Ontario and probably crossed into the region at the west end of Lake Erie after the ice receded. But within the past thirty or forty years another race of bobcat has moved around to the north shore of Lake Superior, entering the region at two places, first around the west end of the lake, then from the upper peninsula of Michigan by way of Cockburn Island near Manitoulin, and from there to the mainland and north along the Superior shore. In recent years the two contingents met, surrounding Lake Superior, and it is predicted that they will work their way around Georgian Bay and into southern Ontario to join the other variety there. Another odd recent migration in the Great Lakes region is that of the thirteen-lined ground squirrel. This animal occurs in the prairies and west of the Detroit and St. Clair Rivers, but Randolph L. Peterson, Curator of Mammology of the Royal Ontario Museum, states that one animal was photographed in July 1959 in Sibley Provincial Park near Port Arthur, Ontario, and that it was "seen several times in the summer of 1959."

A QUARTET OF STRANGE MIGRANTS

 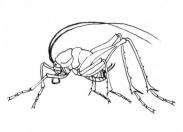 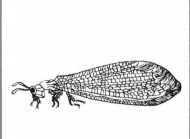 

The 1 in. long rhinoceros beetle looks fierce but is quite friendly. | *Wingless camel crickets are found hidden in dark and humid cavities.* | *Antlions resemble damselflies but fly poorly; their larvae eat ants.* | *Male gay-winged locusts make a clattering noise when they fly.*

14 THE CHANGING WILDLIFE

When the Europeans arrived in the Great Lakes region, the ice had vanished, the mastodons had been extinct for 6,000 years, the lakes looked the way they do today. But dense forests covered their shores, and animals now extinct, and others long gone from the region, inhabited what is now southern Ontario. There were caribou on Georgian Bay as far south as the French River. Martens, the mink-like animals with long bushy tails and big ears, now found only north of the edge of the shield, raced after red squirrels in the tops of the white pines. In the forests around Lake Erie and Lake Ontario cougars stalked deer and pierced the nights with their screams. Buffalo browsed on the southern shore of Lake Erie. Wapiti, a majestic elk with a heavy dark mane, browsed on grasses and shrubs, and wheeled and trotted through the forests. He was a fast runner and attained speeds of forty-five miles an hour (reckoned from studies of closely related existing species).

The passenger pigeon, which looked like a big handsome mourning dove with a blue head and rusty breast, made a clamour in the woods, rustled in the leaves of the forest floor as it searched for beechnuts and acorns, and swept overhead in flocks that blotted out the sun. The size of these flocks are described in *The Passenger Pigeon in Ontario*, Contribution No. 7 of the Royal Ontario Museum, by Margaret H. Mitchell. She quoted one observer, who says that early one day in May near Niagara, (in the 1860s) he saw a flock of birds that he judged to be 300 miles long, estimating from the flying speed of the birds and the duration of the flight. "I was perfectly amazed to behold the air filled, the sun obscured by millions of pigeons, not hovering about, but darting onwards in a straight line with arrowy flight, in a vast mass a mile or more in breadth, and stretching before and behind as far as the eye could reach. . .

"It was late in the afternoon before any decrease in the mass was perceptible, but they became gradually less dense as the day drew to a close. At sunset the detached flocks bringing up the rear began to settle in the forest on the Lake-road, and in such numbers as to break down branches from the trees."

Gradually the land around Lake Ontario and Lake Erie, and the southern part of Lake Huron, was cleared of forests. The wapiti dwindled as the land was cleared. By 1850, there were none in eastern Canada, and not long afterward the race was extinct. Caribou left the Great Lakes completely, except for a small area around the Nipigon district of Lake Superior. The last passenger pigeon was seen at Penetanguishene on May 18, 1902, after about a hundred years of slaughter – probably the most insane slaughter of one particular form of wildlife, that has ever taken place in North America.

The birds were shot, clubbed, netted and trapped for sport, for food and for no reason except that there were so many of them, and they were so easy to catch and kill. They were knocked down from their roosts at night with sticks and clubbed from hilltops when they passed overhead in low flying flocks. They were caught live, to be released for trap-shooting contests. They were wiped out by the millions. This was not the only reason for their extinction. The cultivation of the land wiped out the pigeon's nesting sites. It is this clearing of the Great Lakes forests that has been the biggest factor in the changes of wildlife in the area.

The agricultural land south of the shield is now in many respects so much like the prairies that animals are working their way in from the west. The badger, an animal of open grasslands, has crossed to the north shore of Lake Erie from the American prairies. One of its chief foods on the prairies is the ground squirrel, which does not live east of the head of the lakes. But the badger kills woodchucks and cottontails, after digging them out of their burrows. Since 1900 the coyote has spread into Ontario, and in southern Ontario is interbreeding with dogs so extensively that it is becoming a confused species. A red wolf persistently turns up in reports of southern Ontario, but this is unlikely, because the proper red wolf is a very scarce beast, confined to the lower Mississippi Valley. It could easily be a mixture of a coyote and dog, although some naturalists think it is a subspecies of wolf that has developed in the Great Lakes region.

While some birds and animals withdrew further north as man took over the Great Lakes area, many others have found the settled regions of the Great Lakes, the pastures and small woodlots, roadside hedges, grainfields and city suburbs an ideal environment. The piping plover, a small, shy, shore bird that

No, it's not the Prairies. But the land around Sarnia is so prairie-like that it draws animals from the western region.

builds nests lined with pebbles and bits of shell between the shore and the dunes, has become one of Ontario's scarcest breeding birds, largely because the beaches have been taken over by sun bathers. Yet the killdeer, a plover that likes regions of short grass, has not only found mowed fields to its liking, but has found suburban life made to order, taking advantage of the golf courses, where it likes to nest. Ravens retreated before the advance of civilization, but crows have multiplied enormously since man began to cultivate the Great Lakes region. The crow is an open-country bird that prefers cleared areas with just enough woodland for nesting and roosting. It's a great forager in dumps, and now the food left over by man enables it to winter comfortably in the Great Lakes region. "As far as the crow is concerned," P. A. Taverner wrote in 1937 in *Birds of Canada*, published by the National Museum of Canada, "the primitive 'balance of nature' has been profoundly and irrevocably changed in its favour."

Horned larks find ideal forage among the weeds of airports. Mourning doves inhabit open woods and forage in weedy pastures, cultivated fields and gravel pits. Flickers prefer open woods, farmlands, burnland, and pastures along forests, and have found wooden telephone posts handy nesting places.

Swallows perch like strings of beads along the country telephone wires. Kingbirds, the bright white and black birds usually seen chasing crows, also like open fields, pastures and parklands, with wire fences for perches. Robins find good pickings of angle worms on the well-groomed lawns of commuter homes, and catbirds appreciate the protective cover of the ornamental trees and shrubs.

Some forms of wildlife work right into the city. Barred owls have found city pigeons easy prey. Whenever there's a round-up of pigeons at Toronto's St. Lawrence Market, two or three barred owls are caught in the nets along with them. Grey squirrels were among the first North American animals to adopt city ways, learning to cross city streets on the telephone wires. Skunks now live under warehouses and city homes. Cottontail rabbits raise families on Toronto's subway right-of-way, in a private world of shrubs and grassy slopes near the centre of the city.

The redwinged blackbird formerly nested almost exclusively in marshes, and was seen clinging to the tules, the bulrushes sedges and cattails in the wind; since the draining of many marshes, he has adapted himself to places like the fringe of trees and grass around Havergal College at Avenue Road and Law-

Cardinals raise up to four fledglings in nests of twigs and grass on shrubs and small trees; they began to settle in Ontario in 1901.

Specimens of the passenger pigeon, now extinct, are preserved at the Royal Ontario Museum; they were a common sight a century ago.

rence Avenue, in Toronto. Here he gives his wild, swampy cry within twenty feet of some of the heaviest commuter traffic on the continent. The starling, a European bird, that has multiplied in North America until it numbers tens of millions since 120 were released in New York in 1890-91, finds electric billboards warm roosting sites on cold winter nights. TV antennae make good perches for many birds. The nighthawk lays its eggs on gravel roofs of apartment buildings. Chimney swifts, which originally nested in caves and hollow trees, now find chimneys more convenient.

The city offers a big and ready supply of food for birds and animals. Gulls move uptown from the lakefront to perch on buildings, and when the coast is clear, make raids on exposed garbage. Tall buildings are used as aeries by sparrow hawks. Insects, attracted by street lamps and city signs, provide rich feeding grounds for bats. The big brown bat, which hibernates in the city, often in the attic of private homes, occasionally wakes up on a warm day and crawls into the living quarters of dwellings. One exotic Great Lakes resident that looks as if it's going to stay is the ring-necked pheasant, which was introduced to North America in 1881, when birds from China were liberated in Oregon. It is now especially well established in the 5,500

acres of marsh on Pelee Island, in western Lake Erie.

There have been some important changes in the bird life of the Great Lakes region in recent years. J. L. Baillie, of the Royal Ontario Museum's Department of Ornithology, reported in the September 1967 issue of the *Ontario Naturalist* that the prairie chicken, which before 1900 flourished in southwestern Ontario, has disappeared, except for a small remnant from Manitoulin Island westward, and that the bobwhite which used to range in southern Ontario, north to Muskoka and east to Kingston, are now reduced to only a few in the extreme southwest of Ontario. The redheaded woodpecker has dwindled, partly as a result of the disappearance of the big oak forests, but also because this bird likes to feed on insects along the highways and can't gain altitude quickly enough to avoid fast cars.

The replacing of wooden fence posts with metal ones has been a factor in the drastic reduction of the eastern bluebird, and another factor is competition with the starling for nesting sites. One of the most dramatic changes has been the arrival on the Great Lakes of the great black-backed gull; and yet nobody knows what brought about this change. Before 1954, this bird was a real "sea gull," nesting on the Gulf of St. Lawrence. Since 1954 a few pairs have nested at Presqu'ile on Lake Ontario and on Little Haystack Island in Lake Huron. The common egret began to nest in a colony of black-crowned night herons at East Sister Island, near the western end of Lake Erie, and by 1961 numbered ten pairs. The cattle egret, which originally crossed the Atlantic from Africa to Guyana, and appeared in Florida in 1941, is another new arrival around the Great Lakes.

Birds and animals have been moving north into southern Ontario, with the recent warming trend in the climate. The grasshopper sparrow has worked its way two hundred miles north in a hundred years. The cardinal is one species that keeps extending its range further north in the area. The first Canadian nesting was reported from Point Pelee in 1901. In 1937 P. A. Taverner wrote in *Birds of Canada* "the type form crosses the Canadian border commonly along the western end of Lake Erie, occurring as scattered individuals and in isolated communities, there and in adjoining localities." In 1966, W. Earl Godfrey reported in *The Birds of Canada,* that it breeds and resides throughout the year, north to Owen Sound, Orillia and Tweed, and has been seen as far north as Kirkland Lake. Other southern species, that have recently begun nesting in Ontario, are the mockingbird, turkey vulture, Carolina wren, golden-winged warbler, yellow-breasted chat, Louisiana waterthrush, tufted titmouse, hooded warbler and Bewick's wren.

The opossum is one of the most persistent invaders of the southern part of the Great Lakes region. At least nine opossums were recorded between 1892 and 1906. Then none were reported until 1934, when a single animal was recorded and the opossum seemed to have disappeared from Ontario. But beginning in 1947, it apparently commenced the strongest invasion yet recorded. At least twenty-five adults plus a number of young were reported. In an article in the *Journal of Mammology*, Randolph L. Peterson, author of the *Mammals of Eastern Canada*, and S. C. Downing, put a finger on the weakness of statistical evidence by pointing out, that rather than indicating an increase in the number of opossums in southern Ontario, it may simply mean that there are more opossum watchers. Most of these opossums were found in the winter time, so it may be possible they cross on ice rafts. But the opossum may have another very obvious way of getting across the Great Lakes – by crossing the Rainbow or Peace Bridge at night. Probably it also arrives by modern transport, in shipments of produce.

15 THE ANIMAL COMMUNITY

If lines are drawn across southern Ontario from Sarnia to Hamilton, from Penetang to Kingston, and from Michipicoten on the east shore of Lake Superior to Quebec City, (if extended) the Canadian part of the Great Lakes drainage basin will be divided into four main zones. Many of the birds and mammals inhabit ranges that conform roughly to these zones, which mark off different kinds of region. This is far from being a hard and fast rule, but the division turns up in the range charts of many forms of wild life.

The line from Georgian Bay to Kingston, particularly, which marks the edge of the shield, is a definite boundary for many species. Moose for example, rarely appear south of the shield, except for an occasional stray yearling, chased from the herd in the fall. The moose is an animal of the northern evergreen forests where, in winter, balsam fir constitutes a staple in its diet. This would be a starvation diet for deer, but deer thrives on young poplar and maples that take over after a fire, or when the forest has been cleared for agriculture. The deer also thrives on white cedar, which again would be a starvation diet for a moose. As a result the deer not only occur north of the shield, but throughout the entire Great Lakes region.

The soils around the Great Lakes make a big difference to some smaller animals. The star-nosed mole, although it tunnels deeper than most moles, spends more time above ground. It is a good swimmer, and spends a lot of time foraging for food in bogs and lakes, on the surface or underwater. It can live on the shield, where the soils are shallow, and throughout the entire Great Lakes region, except the very southwest corner. But the eastern mole spends all its life underground, digging tunnels just below the surface of the ground, or digging down to twenty-four inches below the surface grubbing for earthworms and insects. It needs fairly deep soil that is easy to tunnel through. The soil must not have too much clay in it, which can make it as hard as stone, and it cannot be too sandy, as it would keep falling into the burrow. What the eastern mole finds just right, is the soil of the old lake plains of southwestern Ontario along the Erie shore, where this mole is commonly found.

A black tern nests on a pond in May, displaying its black breeding plumage and laying 2 or 3 eggs while the snow is still melting.

The basic structure of beaver dams consists of twigs cemented with mud, reinforced and built up to reach the required water level.

But within these major zones, every kind of terrain has its wildlife communities – the dunes and meadows and second-growth woodlots. There are still big marshes around the Great Lakes shores, a kind of locality that is rapidly disappearing. At Point Pelee there's a board walk that goes out into a big cattail-marsh for two-thirds of a mile, with a raised observation deck at the end. Great blue herons wade out into the water and wait motionless to spear a frog or fish. Rails with their big feet walk over floating lily pads, and the black tern makes its nest on floating mats of rushes. With any luck a fox snake can be spotted. Pelee Point is one of the few places where this snake can still breed in relative safety from man.

A beaver pond is a specialized environment. There is hardly a stream inside Algonquin park without a beaver dam, and some of these can be seen from the roads off Highway 60. All that is needed, to get a first-hand picture of the life of these ponds is patience and the ability to sit still. The high water caused by the beaver dam kills the trees, by cutting off the air from their roots, and in a typical pond dead spruce and balsam fir stick up from the edges of the pond like arrows. These are favourite nesting places for flickers and old rotted-out flicker holes are ready-made homes for wood ducks, which always nest near water. The young downies of the wood duck have needle-sharp claws and climb up to the opening. From there they either jump or get pushed by their mothers into the wide world. They may drop twenty feet and usually alight on the water, but it doesn't seem to matter if they hit dry land, since they are as light as ping-pong balls and just parachute down to the ground.

The meadow mouse likes the wet, grassy shores of the pond, and black ducks come in to bottom-feed there, in preference to the deeper waters of the lakes. Leopard frogs breed in the ponds, and this brings in the garter snake, since frogs are one of its main foods. Muskrats often build their houses in a beaver pond. Painted turtles with yellow-striped, moss-green heads and glimpses of vermillion under the shell, like to sun themselves on a rock or a floating log at the pond's edge.

16 FISHES SWARM INTO THE LAKES

When the glaciers came down over the land, the fresh water creatures retreated to waterways in the south. About 14,000 years ago, when the glaciers began to recede, and waters from their melting ice fronts began to flow down the tributaries of the Mississippi, the fishes began working their way back, up the cold glacial streams. Some species followed the streams right up to the newly formed lakes. Brook trout and lake trout thrive in cold water and they lived close to the receding ice. The northern sucker was another colonist of these new frigid lakes. Some of the species that returned to the region had evolved along different lines since their exodus to the south. The varieties of muskellunge, according to one theory, are the result of two branches of ancestral stock that were driven into separate regions of the Mississippi drainage system, and were then isolated from one another by the advancing ice.

Other forms of life were populating the sterile new lakes. Underwater insects, with suction cups on their under-sides by which they could stick to the upstream side of rocks, began to inhabit rushing glacial streams. Mayflies dropped their eggs to the lake bottom. The Great Lakes presented an enormous new, changing aquatic environment.

As the ice withdrew from the region of the thousand Islands, ocean fish, like the Atlantic salmon, came up into the salt-water gulf. Atlantic salmon congregated in river mouths and migrated up the stream to spawn. As the earth's crust was freed from the weight of the ice, the eastern end of the Ontario basin was slowly rising. The outlet from the Ontario basin became shallower as the land rose, and the salmon were cut off from the sea and adapted themselves to fresh-water. The alewife may also have been landlocked in the same way, but there is some belief that it was introduced to the lakes by a fish culturist on the Genesee River in New York.

Another aquatic animal that found itself isolated from the ocean was the sea lamprey. These animals of the sea, landlocked by the rising channel at the east end of the lake system, were prevented from migrating further west by Niagara Falls.

In pioneer times, salmon were caught in all the rivers that empty into Lake Ontario. More than a thousand were often caught in one stream in a night, and they were sometimes 40 pounds in weight. The Don and the Etobicoke were rich fishing grounds. An announcement in the *Gazette of York* in 1798, advertised a valuable farm with a salmon fishery on Yonge Street. Many farms were paid for by the salmon catch. At Newcastle, Ontario, salmon were so numerous that every autumn, according to one report, women seined them with flannel petticoats. Sturgeon came up all the big rivers to spawn in May or early June. These fish, which can live to be 150 years old (one was caught in 1953 in Lake of the Woods that was born before the battle of Trafalgar, in 1805) grow to a length of eight feet.

Whitefish that often weighed twenty pounds were caught in the lakes. George Bond described the Indians spearing whitefish or possibly lake trout (which he called salmon) at night on Lake Simcoe: "the fish-spear consisted of a straight handle about fifteen feet long, to which a couple of barbed iron spikes, of sufficient size to pierce a moderate salmon were affixed. The birch-bark, for the purpose was prepared in pieces three or four double, each the size of a large quarto book; and one at a time of these was stuck in a cleft pole five or six feet long, placed at the head of the canoe, overhanging the water in such a manner that the blazing bark might shine upon it. The canoe was a very eggshell, cranky as a washing-tub, and more fitted to carrying ghosts than men."

Since the arrival of Europeans in North America there have been changes in the life of the lakes, just as great as the changes on land. Atlantic salmon disappeared from Lake Ontario just before the turn of the century. In the autumn of 1964 the fisheries branch of the Ontario Department of Lands and Forests planted eggs of a small landlocked salmon, called the kokanee, in several places in Georgian Bay and Lake Ontario. By the fall of 1966 hundreds of reports were received of two-year-old salmon being seen or caught from Manitoulin Island to the Bay of Quinte, but it is too early to tell whether they will become permanent residents of the lakes again. Sturgeon were once so numerous throughout the lakes, that they were considered to be pests, that broke fish nets and preyed on more profitable commercial fish. Some were sold as smoked halibut in 1860, but tons of them were brought to the shore and destroyed. This spectacular fish as big as a sand shark has dwindled to a few colonies in the Great Lakes, notably in Lake St. Clair.

The lake trout disappeared from Lake Huron and Michigan following the invasion of the parasitic sea lamprey, which reached the upper lakes from Lake Ontario through the Welland Canal. It had not caused any change in the fish population of Lake Ontario, and it did not do much harm in Lake Erie. The lamprey cannot be blamed for the disappearance of the white-fish from Lake Erie. If it had been the cause, the burbot, a cod-like fish which the lamprey also likes, would have disappeared too, or at least would have dwindled. But it thrived for years after the invasion of the lamprey. Even without the ravages of the lamprey, fish have disappeared from Lake Erie one by one for over a hundred years. Around the 1870s the muskellunge disappeared, then the sturgeon, followed by the northern pike. The smallmouth bass decreased noticeably but, ironically, was saved by being classified a game fish. Because of this it was protected by licence, regulating the size and numbers that could be caught. The lake trout disappeared around 1900.

The freshwater herring, or cisco, one of the important fish since the 1870s, almost died out in 1925, had a brief revival between 1945 and 1947, but now it is not caught anywhere in Lake Erie. By 1940 the whitefish were gone. The greatest changes in Lake Erie have taken place since the 1940s. In some respects the changes have coincided with pollution and the resulting over-production of algae and increased sedimentation. Lake Erie lies in one of the most heavily industrialized parts of North America and in an area of rapidly increasing human population. But drastic changes have also been caused by an unregulated fishing industry, and introduction of fish to the lakes by man, as pointed out by Dr. H. A. Regier, of the Department of Zoology, University of Toronto. The two fishes accounting for nearly all the catch now in Lake Erie are the yellow perch and the smelt, originally an ocean fish, which spread throughout the lakes from a planting of eggs in Lake Michigan in 1912.

The muskellunge, a fighting member of the pike family, inhabits the margins and tributaries of lakes. Feeding voraciously on small fish, he can reach a length of five feet, and a weight of 70 lb.

The lake sturgeon (top) with bony plates along its body and an ancestry of 100 million years, feeds on lake bottoms with the smaller whitefish – reduced in numbers by lampreys and pollution.

The sauger, often confused with the walleye (bottom drawing), shows black dots along the dorsal fin.

The blue pike, another relative, differs in its rate of growth, time of spawning and size (13 inches). It has almost disappeared.

The walleye itself has an elongated and robust body, misted eyes and a brown colouring speckled with gold. It can grow up to 23 pounds.

17 THE VANISHING LAKE ERIE WALLEYE

In an earlier chapter it was pointed out that plants and animals had been placed in separate sections of this book only for reference, and that there were no such convenient compartments of nature. All forms of life are interdependent. A plant or animal exists within a complex framework, called by biologists a niche. This means much more than living *in* a certain region, or corner of that region. It is not hard to see that a woodchuck needs a place to dig a burrow, or that a red squirrel would be sadly displaced if it were taken away from the woods. A niche is a much more subtle and finely balanced set of relationships, involving not only the physical surroundings, but the particular role an animal plays within the rest of the animal community, enabling it to live in harmony with its environment.

The habitat of a fish is a lake, or a particular bay or river and, at first thought, it seems about all that it needs. Give a fish a lake and some food, and it couldn't ask for more. The fact is it is doomed if it doesn't get a great deal more, including the precise balance of light and temperature and oxygen; the right spawning grounds, currents, freedom of movement, the right balance of other fish populations: if these things are thrown out of balance, as they often are, particularly by man, an entire species, or a whole system of animal population, may disappear. This is what will happen, unless something is done about it, to the western Lake Erie walleye, which now seems to be in line as the next victim of this biological disaster area.

The walleye, also called the pike perch, pickerel and, in early days, the doré, a word derived from the French for "gold" is an olive-brown and brassy yellow fish with prickly scales, glassy eyes and the general appearance of a long perch. It grows two and a half feet long or more, and sometimes lives for twenty years in waters that aren't too heavily fished. It is closely related to two other fish that inhabit Lake Erie, or did until a few years ago – the blue pike and the sauger – both so closely resembling the walleye that the three are sometimes confused. These three species of fish are believed to have descended from a European member of the family that found its way from Asia to North America.

Whatever their origin, the walleye, sauger and blue pike were fished by spear, nets, weir and hook and line in Lake Erie from 1815 to the 1900s, when the fish populations in Lake Erie began to change. In 1910 the blue pike population began to vary from abundance to scarcity, and by 1959 only stray individuals were caught in Lake Erie. Since then it has almost disappeared. The sauger had a peak year in 1921, then it too began to diminish. There have been virtually none in the lake since about 1957. The walleye increased as the sauger decreased, until in 1956, Lake Erie fishermen had the biggest catch in history; then it began to decline. The walleye catch, which had averaged about seven million pounds a year in the 1940s, dropped to one million pounds in the early 1960s and since then has continued to decrease (to 328,411 pounds in 1968).

The walleye spawns in water from 38 to 44 degrees Fahrenheit, usually soon after the ice goes out in April or May. It spawns on gravelly or sandy bottoms, sometimes on shoals of the lake, but usually in streams. Large schools swim upstream, the males usually preceding the females, but sometimes one female will be escorted by several males. The walleye spawns at night in rapids where the stream gurgles down over a bouldery bottom. A five-pound female lays about 100,000 eggs. The eggs float downstream until they stick to the gravel bottom, where they take two or three weeks to hatch. Walleyes, as do most fish, spawn on sandy and pebbly bottoms partly because, if laid on mud bottoms, the eggs would be in danger of dying from lack of oxygen. The walleye needs water almost saturated with oxygen. On muddy and oozy bottoms, the oxygen is depleted by bacteria, which uses it to break down the molecules of decaying matter.

Many fish are very fastidious in the matter of avoiding mud bottoms when they spawn. Largemouth bass will deposit eggs on tufts of grass and roots and any cleaned-off submerged vegetation rather than on the surrounding mud. The male of the smallmouth bass prepares a nest by fanning the bottom with his tail, cleaning away the silt and sand until he has a saucer-shaped nest two to three feet across made of clean stones, and he works so hard at it that he may take several days at the job. When pebble bottoms become covered with silt, as they have in almost all streams around Lake Erie, the silt partly fills the spaces between the stones. The walleye eggs, instead of settling

Will pollution rob the walleye of its spawning grounds? This school ascends a clear stream, but most lake tributaries are now silted up.

to clean sand between the stones, lie on mud. Not only that, they are in a relatively raised position and more easily found and picked up by egg-eating fish. They are also easily washed out of the crevices onto even less suitable bottoms. When this happens the spawning grounds are abandoned. Perhaps the instinct that prevents the walleye from laying eggs on mud warns her off. Perhaps the walleye can no longer find enough suitable grounds.

It is not known how the walleye, or any other fish, finds its way back to its birthplace to spawn, but it may be by a sense of smell. A particular river, shoal or stretch of rapids has a certain bouquet that leads the fish there. When the shoal or the river changes through silting, or when it becomes covered with underwater growth from chemical enrichment of the water, this smell is masked, and the walleye becomes a displaced individual, wandering with spawning schools of other species of fish.

Another thing that may drive the walleye from its own territory is increasing turbidity of the water. The vision of the adult walleye is adapted to dim light. During hours of bright sunlight, walleyes generally stay in waters that are slightly murky either from sediment or aquatic plant life, or move out into deeper water, or into the shade of rocks, logs or weeds. Scuba divers say that in the daytime they see walleyes lying motionless on the bottom in western Lake Erie. The walleye rises off the bottom at sunset to feed. It is relatively quiet during the night. At dawn it becomes active again. But although the walleye doesn't like too much light, it is a sight feeder. The walleye when young feeds mostly on plankton and later on insects like the mayfly nymph. But as an adult it hunts perch and minnows and suckers and it relies on seeing its prey. If the water is too cloudy the walleye is a very inefficient hunter. It needs enough turbidity to dim the sunlight during the day, but enough light, so it can find its prey. It is a precisely balanced condition.

Any change in these factors, the silting of spawning beds, a change in turbidity of the water, can cause the walleye to abandon certain regions. In an odd way the dwindling of suitable spawning and feeding areas reverses the process of evolution. Two species of fish have developed along separate lines for many thousands of years, breeding in different types of bay, river mouth or shoals, in waters of different chemical composition. Each has adapted to a particular set of conditions. Because of this, one has become completely different biologically, from the other. But as one spawning ground after another is eliminated by sedimentation, pollution of the water by chemicals, or by other causes, such as barriers of nets, fish migrate seeking other spawning grounds.

As good spawning grounds become scarce, different species of fish mingle, and get trapped in each other's breeding schools by their instinct to spawn. In this way they interbreed. But by this time they have become so different through evolution that they can't produce fertile young. This has been found in the experimental interbreeding of the walleye and sauger in a fish hatchery. A female sauger and male walleye yielded no surviving young. A male sauger and female walleye produced only a few healthy young. Dr. Regier has suggested that interbreeding may have been one of the factors in the virtual disappearance of these closely related but distinct Lake Erie species – the sauger, the blue pike and walleye.

There's hardly a habit of the walleye that hasn't been interfered with in the past fifty years or so. One of the biggest changes has been caused by the overproduction of plant growth as a result of pollution. Every river that it spawns in has become polluted and silted over. Fishermen report that between Middle Sister and East Sister Islands, at depths of about thirty feet, the bottom, which was clean twenty years ago, is now covered with soft ooze that they call fluff. Another change has been the introduction to the lakes, by man, of new species of fish. The walleye's niche in the system of life in the lake has been encroached upon.

While coping with these changes, the walleye has been overfished. Overfishing does not simply mean taking too many fish from the lake, although it can mean this too; it means that fish are taken at the wrong time, in the wrong place, and in a way that completely disrupts their spawning and hunting grounds and their capacity to maintain their species.

A voracious diving beetle larva, known as the water tiger, is caught on the prowl (magnified fifteen times).

MINIATURE MONSTERS

With the aid of a magnifying lens – and infinite patience – Helen Sutton, a gifted
Canadian naturalist-photographer, captures the violent underwater life of the
relatively small number of insects, partly adapted to life under water, that cling
to the element from which most of their kind emerged millions of years ago.

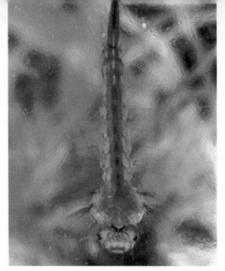

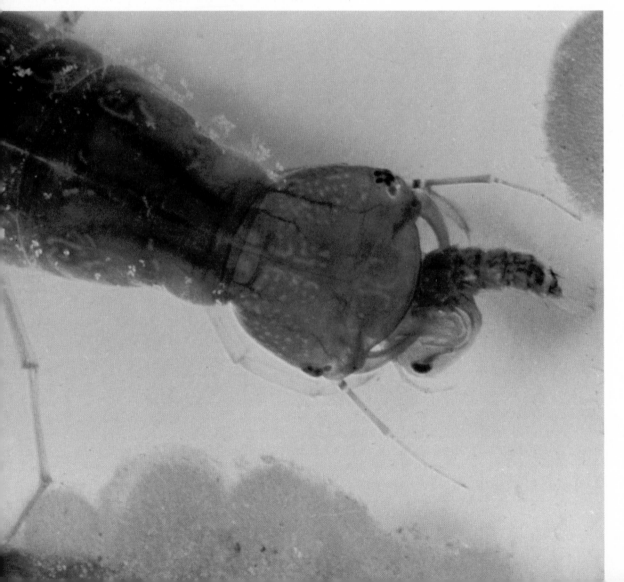

The diving beetle larva searches for a meal . . .   *Its favourite food, a mosquito larva.*

Predator and prey

The larva of the dytiscid diving beetle is as fierce and carnivorous as the fully-grown insect. Lurking among the plants near the edge of the water, its favourite pose is to remain still, with its two breathing tubes broaching the surface, mandibles spread out ready to pounce on its prey. Once within range, the larva darts forward to clutch unwary victims between its sickle-shaped jaws. It sucks out the body-fluid from the prey without having to open its mouth – the hollow jaws act as drinking straws. This larva is commonly known as the water tiger and is abundant in pools and backwaters of streams overgrown with weeds. The adult beetle reaches a length of one inch.

Seizing a mosquito pupa, strong jaws hold the prey while sucking its juices.

1 The mosquito pupa extends a pair of breathing tubes.

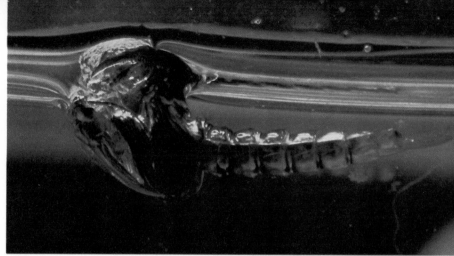

2 The fully developed insect bursts out of its casing.

3 Now the mosquito struggles to free its delicate body.

4 The mosquito rests, permitting its wings to harden.

Birth of a mosquito

Mosquitoes are born from eggs which are laid in still water. The larvae hatching from these eggs are commonly known as wrigglers. They feed on minute plant and animal cells, frequently coming to the surface for air. They soon turn into pupae which look like commas suspended from the surface, until finally the adult mosquito emerges. Only the female sucks your blood.

The huge eyes and menacing lower lip of the dragonfly nymph (magnified twelve times) menace unwary pond dwellers.

A dragon grows wings

The nymph of the dragonfly lives on the muddy bottoms of ponds and small streams, stalking its prey with an ambling gait, prepared to lunge with lightning speed at anything that moves. It catches food by shooting out its lower lip, preferring mayflies, minute crustaceans and snails to other small insects. When ready to hatch, it crawls up a stem and above the water sheds its nymphal skin to emerge as a weak, delicate dragonfly. When you see them in summer circling the surface of the water at the edge of a stream in regular patterns, they are scooping insects from the air with their hairy legs and chewing them with their strong jaws. The female lays her eggs by skimming the surface of the water, dipping her abdomen to deposit the eggs on aquatic plants or sand.

This dragonfly nymph has recently moulted (see old skin).

An adult dragonfly emerges from its chrysalis, wings still captive.

Hovering ready for flight, the insect discards its ghostly case.

Larva of a hydropsychid caddisfly (Magnified twelve times) ventures out of shelter, assembled from material at hand.

A pupa swims to the surface, then changes to a flying insect.

An adult caddisfly awaits the dusk before setting off in flight.

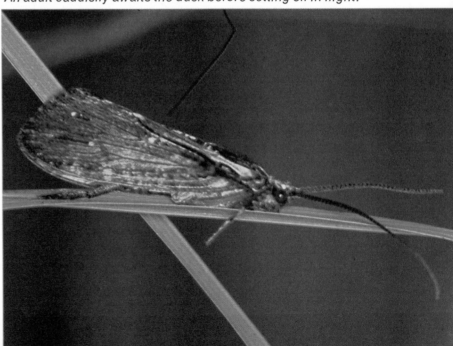

Underwater artists

Caddisflies are delicate moth-like insects with long antennae and often beautiful markings on their wings. They are seldom seen during the day, but their larvae, commonly known as caddis worms, abound in ponds and streams. These "worms" are among the most ingenious architects in nature. With saliva excreted from their bodies they build cocoons with a bewildering variety of materials found on the bottom of ponds and streams. Different species specialize in a range of materials from leaves and twigs to shells and stones arranged in snail-shaped, tubular and even rectangular patterns. Some species construct intricate nets in order to trap their prey. They move about by gripping the casing with claws attached to their abdomen – the head and legs protrude from the front. Like all aquatic insects the larvae develop gills for under-water breathing and when they are ready to hatch, swim or crawl to the surface to emerge as flies, living for a month.

Reed and grass strips make a home for this larva.

How the caddis larva builds its house

The silken thread produced by caddis worms is similar to that woven into a cocoon by moths. It serves not only as a building material, but also as an interior lining. The three photographs on this page all show the types of homes constructed by the larvae.

This caddis larva builds its case in horizontally-knit layers.

Shells, bark, seeds and pebbles protect this caddis larva.

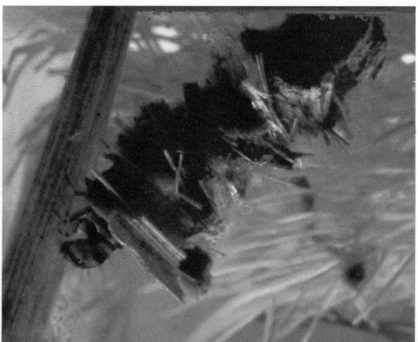

The sting of death

The water scorpion carries a fatal poison in its rapier-like proboscis. It resembles a stick insect but is a slender water-bug up to one-and-a-quarter inches long. It crawls through the vegetation and trash of the shallow lake bottom, with a long respiratory tube protruding from the abdomen. The nymph looks very much like the adult and is equally voracious, feeding on all forms of invertebrate life by sucking out the body-fluids. The strong front legs are well adapted for holding the victim, allowing the sturdy proboscis to bore into the tissue. A favourite pose is to hang like a dead stick suspended from the surface, ready to pounce on any insect within range. The water scorpion is insatiable and it has been observed to greedily clutch and suck dry one mayfly after another.

◀ *A water scorpion tries—and fails—to pierce the hard casing of a water beetle.*

The syringe-like proboscis of the water scorpion projects from its freakish head.

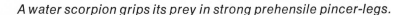

A water scorpion grips its prey in strong prehensile pincer-legs.

Holding its victim—a mosquito larva—the scorpion sucks it dry.

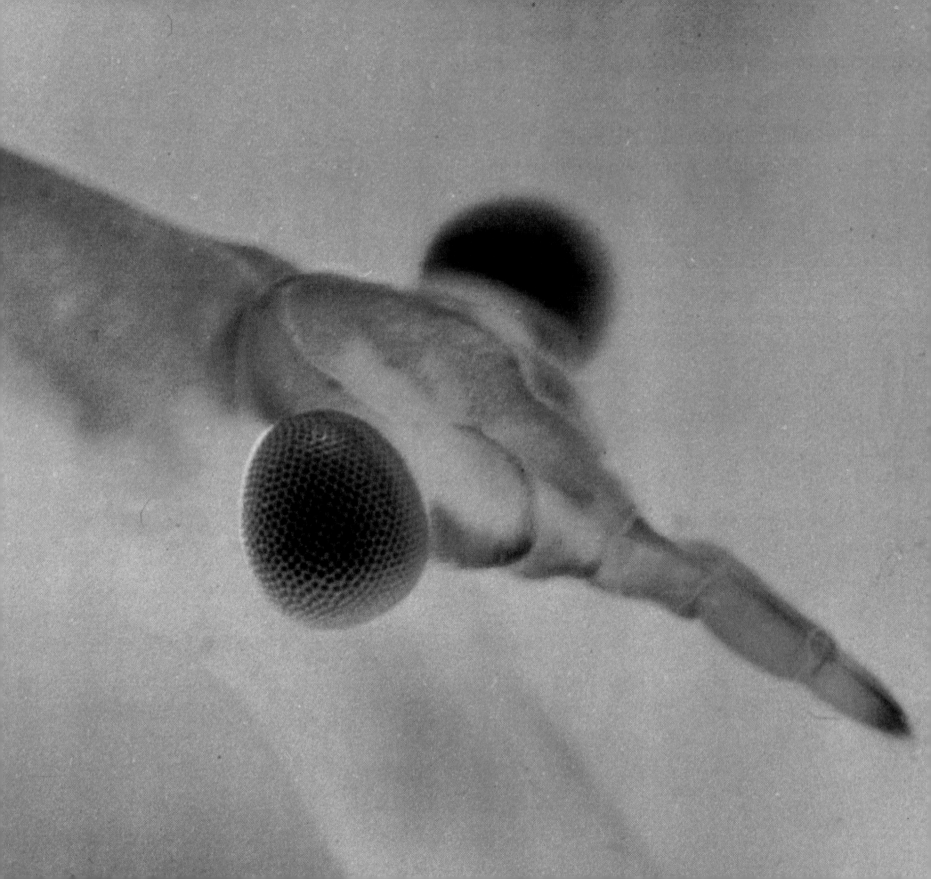

The mayfly nymph is distinguishable by its forked tail filaments.

Leaf-like gills (much magnified) filter out oxygen.

In its final fragile beauty, the adult mayfly lasts but a few hours.

To mate and die

The life of the mature mayfly is brief — usually a few hours — never more than three days. As though called by a mysterious signal, they ascend from the water to perform a mad dance in dense swarms of thousands. The female is fertilized in flight, descends to the water, lays about 4,000 eggs and dies shortly afterwards. The adult never eats, but the nymph feeds on microscopic plants and rotting vegetation, during its two-year growth; it sheds its skin up to twenty times in this period. Mayfly nymphs are in constant danger of being caught by small fish and predatory dragonfly nymphs, often serving as their main diet. Yet, many survive to emerge from the water as "duns." In this state they have taken their final form but, unlike any other insect, they still must shed another gossamer skin to take their final shape as "spinners," perform the mating ritual, and perish.

A mayfly nymph can live only in fresh water, where it feeds on . . . the smallest living plants and rotting vegetation.

This apparently perfect mayfly, complete with wings, is in fact, the "dun" of the insect; it will soon shed its gossamer skin.

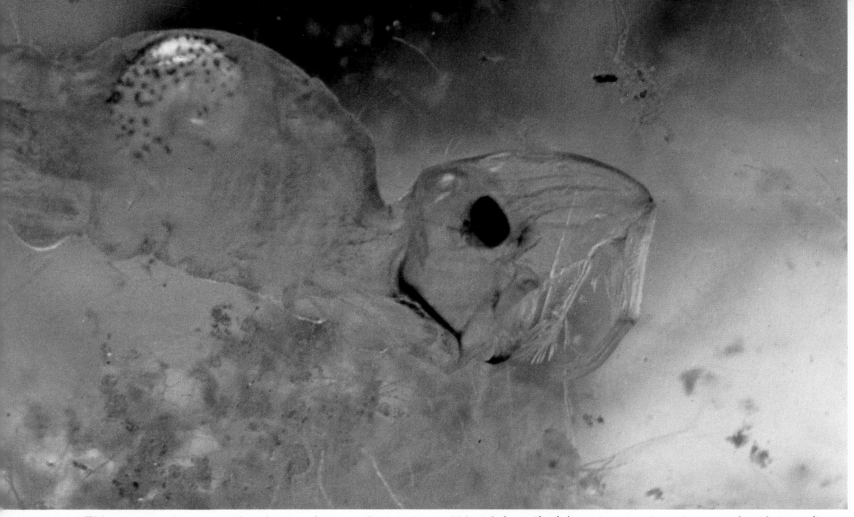

This creature, known as the phantom larva – a flesh eater – will hatch from the lakewaters as a harmless species of mosquito.

Transparent life

The details of many forms of underwater life are too minute to be seen with the naked eye, particularly if they are transparent. Present wherever life exists, these planktonic creatures – a diet for small fishes – form a vital link in the food chain that, in the end, enables man himself to exist.

This water-flea – a crustacean, not an insect – is here seen with a number of eggs within its frail body. This prolific "flea" can produce a new brood every two days.

PART FIVE / A FIELD TRIP

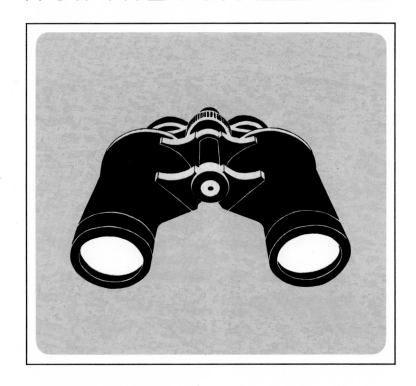

18 THE FORGOTTEN LAND

The Bruce Peninsula, a rugged fifty-mile jetty of rock, forest and rough farmland dividing Lake Huron from Georgian Bay, lies at the heart of the Great Lakes like some lingering memory of a distant geological age. Its very surface rocks are coral reefs and limestone sediments deposited beneath ancient seas. The headlands of its eastern shore, formed by the Niagara Escarpment, lie brooding over Georgian Bay.

As if nature herself held to this link with the past, parts of the peninsula are the wildest in southern Ontario. Sections of its eastern shore are almost inaccessible except by water. Eagles coast its swamps and dunes. Black bears den-up in limestone caves that were there before man arrived in North America. The lynx-eyed Massasauga rattler basks amid slender walking-ferns that spread a green net over fallen rocks on the eastern shore. In the marshy regions between the sand dunes on the Lake Huron shore are strange isolated pockets of flowers that have been there since the ice age, and rare orchids that die if transplanted to city gardens.

In winter, the shores of the Bruce are a bleak, icy wilderness. At Sauble Beach, a busy resort in summer, frozen blocks of ice, bearded with icicles, hang a foot above the slush ice of the sombre heaving water. Against a dark green backdrop of cedar and tamarack, a lone snowshoe hare, startled from its refuge in the frozen dunes, bolts through the winter twilight, beneath the blind stare of the boarded-up cottages. The water freezes in fanciful forms. Some parts of the beach are paved with round balls of ice, shaped like cobbles. In the silence of a winter afternoon the ice makes muffled snapping sounds like branches being snapped in a distant bog, and sometimes moans as if dreaming restlessly of the days when it conquered half the earth. Deer trample out their yards amid the cedar-topped dunes and beach-side cottages, spreading a coat of manure over the frozen petunia beds beneath department-store lanterns and a sad, frozen sign reading *Dun Rovin'*. Sometimes, when a sick or wounded animal has succumbed to the cold or infection, coyotes have picked the bones clean and left them to bleach on a cottage lawn.

This secluded retreat extends from the southern end of Geor-

gian Bay. The base of the peninsula is a line between Owen Sound on Georgian Bay and the town of Southampton on Lake Huron, but the more typical landscape of the Bruce begins at the town of Wiarton, where Colpoy Bay, a deep indentation of the eastern shore, almost pinches the peninsula into an island. From there Highway 6 goes fifty miles northwest in long straight stretches to the town of Tobermory which is located at the toe of this inverted boot, almost like an upside-down Italy. The land is straight and flat. At intervals, the horizon to the right is stamped with the familiar chunky profile of the escarpment weaving its way up the eastern shore.

Very little of the Bruce, particularly the northern part, is cultivated. The farms are devoted mostly to grazing cattle, and the rubble-strewn fields are among the most forbidding, agriculturally, of any land south of the Precambrian Shield. Although there is one area about half-way up the peninsula near Lion's Head where the soil is made up of the silts and clays of a glacial lake, for the most part the soil is scanty and in many areas there are expanses of rough, bare, fissured rock pavement. Blocks of dolomite in the rough farmlands are a reminder that this whole peninsula is a table of rock, slanting gently from east to west. On the western shore the rock pavements slide gradually under Lake Huron, in a region of flat marshy cedar swamps and shallow bays. Along much of the western coastline, ridges of sand dunes parallel the shore. On the east coast the side roads wind down off the escarpment to the few settlements below. At almost every point on the bluff there is a view across the blue water of a bay towards headlands of the escarpment. There are small lakes throughout the peninsula and in the northern part particularly, dense tracts of mixed woods.

The Bruce is located within easy range of week-end cottagers from the most heavily populated regions of the Great Lakes, and already in many areas cottage communities crowd beneath its bluffs and along its sand dunes. In places power boats violate one of the increasingly rare regions of clean, clear water, and, in winter, skidoos disturb the silence and serenity of the woods. Land developers have claimed the western shore except for three hundred acres of beach, woods and marshland at Dorcus Bay, which were salvaged from a bankrupt operator by an astute Owen Sound conservationist and taken over as a nature preserve by the Federation of Ontario Naturalists.

In spite of encroaching civilization, the Bruce Peninsula remains, to date, relatively unspoiled. There are few roads, and some of these are picturesque pioneer style side-roads just wide enough for one car, with buttercups growing right up to the road's edge. The best way to see the Bruce Peninsula is on foot, and a unique opportunity to walk the entire length of the peninsula, through its most scenic, untouched reaches is provided by the Bruce Trail, a 480-mile hiking trail that follows the Niagara Escarpment to Tobermory. It will probably some day link up with the Finger Lakes Trail system of New York State and, through this, with the Appalachian Trail, providing a two-thousand-mile footpath from the State of Georgia to the top of Georgian Bay. The Bruce is the last and most spectacular leg of the trail.

The hike south starts at a cairn at the water's edge of Tobermory and the first part follows the shore east for about four miles to Dunks Bay. This is the last access point to the trail for thirty miles. Although this region is in southern Ontario, and therefore a walk through its woods is apt to be regarded as something comparable with a rather rough hike through a city park, the Bruce Trail guide book emphasizes that it should not be taken too casually. "It is no use undertaking to hike from Dunks Bay to Cabot Head unless you are fully equipped with tent, food and cooking facilities. It takes a well prepared, experienced and fit hiker three days to hike this stretch. You are strongly advised not to attempt this section unless you have consulted with the local people and are properly equipped for the expedition. Do not attempt it alone."

The trail winds and turns so much that mileages are difficult to calculate and hiking times almost impossible to predict. In some areas the hiker will cover less than two miles in an hour. The trail follows the top of the cliffs, often dropping down to water level and rising in places where the line of the cliffs drops back from the shore. The trail rounds Cabot Head at the far northeastern point of the peninsula – 309 feet of sheer, solid rock facing Georgian Bay – and then cuts back southwest to Dyer Bay. A road dips down from the bluffs to a village on the shore. In a significant commentary on this part of the Great Lakes the Bruce Trail guide points out that "good drinking water is available here a few feet out from shore." At several points on the trail hikers are advised to fill up their canteens with drinking water. Many places up on top of the escarpment have no water, and the clear water of Georgian Bay, in full view below, is out of reach at the base of sheer three-hundred-foot cliffs, so that a hiker may go thirsty and yet be able to toss a stone into the greatest supply of fresh water on earth.

The trail follows old logging roads in places and there are side trails to special viewing-points. One leads to a peculiar isolated tower of rock shaped by water and wind, called a "flower pot" which looks more like a giant stone carrot being pulled out of the ground. The trail cuts through dense bush in places. There's a section near Owen Sound that contains almost every variety of tree found in Canada. There are also limestone caves along the trail; one of these is near Oxenden, on the south side of Colpoy Bay. The trail here goes through thick woods at the foot of the escarpment, then climbs part way up the cliffs. Bruce's Caves are enormous recesses in the limestone rock, where the ceiling is supported by natural rock pillars. The sloping floor is covered by blocks of dolomite. A hiker can build a fire here from cedar branches and sit looking out on a rough tangle of rock and woods, and come close to the feeling of what life must have been like for his ancestors – perhaps half a million years ago, during the interval between ice ages.

The Bruce Trail trends generally southeast following the Niagara Escarpment, a rugged natural shelf that coils through southern Ontario, exposing its geological history. The trail leads through maple woods and across gentle farmlands. It traverses the Blue Mountains at Collingwood and skirts Beaver Valley, one of the ancient pre-glacial valleys of the Great Lakes region, eroded out of the escarpment during hundreds of millions of years before the ice age. It cuts through the rolling moraines of Caledon, and overlooks spectacular views of the Ontario countryside from the top of the escarpment. It crosses streams, passes gorges and falls that cascade down over the escarpment, and due to the skilful plotting of the trail organizers, provides a wild natural path right through the city of Hamilton at the west end of Lake Ontario. In places the hiker can look down from a wooded cliff onto city streets and the steel mills and shipping of Hamilton harbour. From Hamilton the trail crosses the fruitlands of the Niagara Peninsula to its southern end at Queenston, located fittingly where the Niagara exposes the bedrock of southern Ontario like the open pages of an ancient book.

Flowerpot Island, three miles from Tobermory, is famed for its pedestal formations, moulded by ancient seas from Devonian rock.

Similar rock pillars support the roof of Bruce's Caves, hewn by water action in the limestone cliffs at Colpoy Bay, near Oxenden.

19 THE ROCKS OF THE BRUCE

The rock structure of the Bruce Peninsula was born at the bottom of a sea. It is part of the Niagara Escarpment, and like all of that ragged, wandering edifice, it is composed of deposits hundreds of millions of years old – the sediments of river deltas, the clays and muds that were carried far out to sea, the lime of the seashells and reefs built by colonies of marine animals. Many exposures of rock on the Bruce Peninsula are due partly to the reefs that formed in this region, much as they do in today's southern seas. At Wiarton, Highway 6 climbs through a cut in a knobby, solid mass of limestone left by teeming colonies of marine creatures. The rocks of the Bruce – those near the Wiarton road-cut, the Kemble road-cut, the Owen Sound-Chatsworth highway, the village of Colpoy, Purple Valley and Lion's Head, to name a few locations – contain fossils of dozens of forms of sea life that inhabited the sand and mud in the seas of the time; stone ghosts of creatures that lived aeons ago.

When the seas withdrew from the continent, they exposed a coastal plain that had once been the sea bottom. This plain sloped from east to west in a way that exposed the edges of layers of hard and soft rocks to rain and wind and the work of rivers that then flowed over the plain. Great limestone blocks tumbled as rivers undercut the softer underlying shales, and in time – 200 to 300 million years ago – the giant step of the Niagara Escarpment divided the Great Lakes region.

The process that created it can still be seen on the Bruce Peninsula, where the profile of the escarpment is, typically, a jumble of massive limestone blocks, a steep face, a flat top gently sloping away from the cliff – a characteristic wrinkle of great age on the face of southern Ontario. Not only were streams cutting back the face of the escarpment, they also flowed over its face to join the main drainage system of what is now the Great Lakes basin. These streams cut notches into the vertical face of the cliff and etched deep valleys out of the rock plain. Two major valleys of this kind, concealed by the waters of Georgian Bay, now provide the deep harbours of Owen Sound and Wiarton.

In those remote pre-Great Lakes times, what is now the Bruce Peninsula was simply a segment of the Niagara Escarpment arising from the surrounding land, just as it does today throughout much of southern Ontario. But a tremendous force further moulded the escarpment and left the lakes behind in relatively recent times. A million years ago, or even more recently, when the glaciers invaded the continent, a wall of ice a mile deep advanced year by year towards the rock bastion of the escarpment.

At the relatively late stage when the ice had retreated from the peninsula, an enormous lake extended from Lake Simcoe to Green Bay, Wisconsin; this was glacial Lake Algonquin. As the level of this lake dropped, following the exposure by the ice of lower outlets, wave action and currents swept the rock face of the Bruce Peninsula clean. As the water fell further, the peninsula emerged like the back of a great crocodile, its high points emerging first, forming a series of islands. At a lower level the action of the waves of this ancient glacial lake cut into the face of the escarpment to create the limestone caves of the cliffs. The pounding surf also produced the peculiar columns of rock like the one south of Lion's Head and those of Flowerpot Island, wearing away their softer rocks and turning out the columns like a great lathe.

When the water of Lake Algonquin began to drain through Lake Nipissing and the outlet to the Mattawa Valley at North Bay, the lake dropped to an extremely low level. At this stage (about 9,500 years ago) it is called Lake Stanley, and it may have been possible to walk right along the escarpment to Manitoulin Island. This would be possible today if Georgian Bay dropped about 120 feet. The lake bottom north of the Bruce Peninsula is the site of extensive scientific investigation today. The escarpment has been traced from soundings and the exploration by skin divers beneath the surface of the water, revealing the same characteristic contours as those of the exposed section. It is a very high escarpment in this submerged region. If Georgian Bay dried up, the north shore of the Bruce would be an escarpment nearly eight hundred feet high, a towering cliff about five times the height of Niagara Falls.

There were several "Niagara Falls" pouring over the escarpment that is now hidden beneath the waters of Georgian Bay, but it is not known whether these were part of a drainage system of Lake Stanley or whether they were much older pre-glacial falls. This cliff, part of the same step of rock that forms the escarpment of the Niagara and Bruce peninsulas extends in a wide arc, its high points visible as the many small islands north of the peninsula, to emerge as the escarpment again at Manitoulin, Cockburn, Drummond and St. Joseph Islands. The same limestone rocks follow a semi-circle through the peninsula of upper Michigan and the west shore of Lake Michigan. The Bruce has a counterpart three hundred miles away in Wisconsin in the Door Peninsula between Green Bay and Lake Michigan.

The sequence of rocks that is exposed on the escarpment of the Bruce Peninsula is an extension of those visible at the Niagara Gorge, with important differences. Many of the Niagara formations come to an end as the escarpment is traced northward and are therefore missing from the peninsula. The Whirlpool formation, for instance, pinches out near Collingwood. The red and green Queenston shale, the same formation – composed of the muds of a great ancient delta – that can be seen in the Niagara Gorge at Queenston, is visible at Owen Sound, on the east side of the Bay.

The dominant rocks of the Bruce are the Amabel and Guelph formations. The Amabel is a continuation, slightly different in composition, of the Lockport dolomite that is seen at the brink of Niagara Falls. It can be seen on the grade near Wiarton where Highway 6 cuts through this rock. The Guelph formation, which again appears in the rapids just above Niagara Falls, can also be seen north of the Wiarton road-cut above the level of the Campbell Monument.

Between the lower Queenston shale and the capping rocks of Amabel and Guelph dolomite, going upward, are first, the Manitoulin formation, a brown dolomite that weathers grey, visible on the east side of the bay at Owen Sound, followed by the Cabot Head formation, fifty-one feet of a soft, red and green shale. Above the Cabot Head rocks in the Dyer Bay dolomite; the Wingfield formation, a thirty-two foot bed of dolomite and shale; and the St. Edmunds dolomite. Dyer Bay dolomite can be seen a mile north of the bay. The other three formations are visible at Rocky Bay, three miles west of Cabot Head lighthouse on the north shore. On top of these strata is the Fossil Hill formation, twelve to twenty-two feet of dolomite containing an abundance of fossils, which can be seen at Isthmus Bay and north of Lion's Head.

The sweeping action of Lake Algonquin, which left the

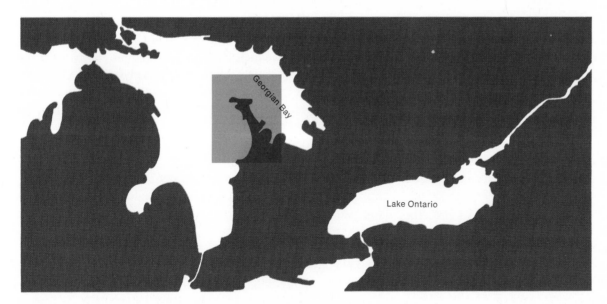

Georgian Bay

Lake Ontario

*A SANCTUARY
IS THREATENED*

*Defying civilization close to
the centre of the Great Lakes,
the Bruce Peninsula harbours a
variety of rare plants, birds,
mammals and reptiles that may
soon disappear from the region.*

Bruce relatively free of glacial deposits, and the coral mounds that are part of the peninsula's structure, resulted in great areas of exposed rock. Strewn over this surface are rounded and pinkish boulders of a kind of rock obviously different from the rough, wrinkled and sometimes pitted, grey rocks of the escarpment. These boulders are erratics – chunks of granite which were pried by the glaciers from the Precambrian Shield to the north – used as grinding tools on the escarpment and strewn over its surface when the glacier retreated.

All rivers but one on the Bruce Peninsula flow west. Some of the rivers form spectacular falls. One of these is located on the Pottawatomi River within view of Highway 21, west of Owen Sound, where the Bruce Trail crosses the road just east of Springmount. These are beautiful falls and a fantastic sight in winter. Frost and mist freeze on stratified rock that looks like an enormous stone mantelpiece. Ice hangs from branches like crystals on a chandelier. Spray and flecks of spume fly up from the base of the falls. It is a busy, fierce sight in the sunny winter woods. At the village of Hepworth there is an underground river which villagers claim they can hear beneath their houses on quiet nights. From its headwaters at Mountain Lake to the northeast it flows about six miles, then goes underground for two miles, emerges as a cold stream inhabited by brook trout, and flows into the Sauble River.

20 A REGION OF RARE PLANTS

The homesteaders and lumber companies of the 1800s went through the forests of the Bruce Peninsula the same way they did through the rest of southern Ontario, taking out the big trees and leaving desolate areas of stumps, rocks and slash. There are none of the big original pines left on the peninsula, and much of the land is completely cleared. Yet there are wild areas of dense woods, particularly in the more remote northern part. The native growth of the Bruce is that of the Great Lakes – St. Lawrence forest region, a mixture of evergreens, such as hemlock, and the broad-leaved trees, such as maple and beech.

There is a definite dividing line about half-way up the peninsula, north of which the forest is that of a transition zone between the mixed forest and the boreal forest region north of the Great Lakes. In this transition zone of the northern peninsula are an increasing number of conifers, such as spruce, red and white pine and jack pine. Everywhere along the shores of the Bruce are twisted ancient gnarled white cedars which thrive on a limestone terrain. In the northern regions of the western shore, at Dorcus Bay, for instance, there are scrubby flats where mullein stands as high as a man and there are flat open areas of pitted limestone rubble covered with sparse, stunted cedars that have the look of the timber line in the Arctic.

Farther south on this shore, near Sauble Beach, there is a beautiful patch of relatively untouched forest, called Walker's Woods, a thick grove of beech, maple, hemlock, gleaming white birch, and such a rich natural growth of tree species that it is regarded as hallowed territory by naturalists, including botanists and ornithologists from the United States who crowd there every summer. Naturalists are now urging the Provincial Government to buy these woods before the cottage developers do. Walking through this forest in winter is like stepping out of our world. The snow is laced with snowshoe rabbit tracks glazed by the sun in sheltered corners. Chickadees perch in the pale sunlight and downy woodpeckers dart around the birch trees, their faint tapping just enough to deepen the silence of the woods.

The most unusual feature of the Bruce is its population of plants. It is difficult to keep from thinking in terms of a "lost continent" when talking of this peculiar spit of land. It presents some baffling pockets of plant life, fragments of flora that stayed behind when the glaciers pulled back farther north. Some plants survive here in isolated colonies separated by thousands of miles from others of their kind. The Alaska orchid, a slender inconspicuous plant grows only on the Bruce Peninsula, Anticosti Island in the Gulf of St. Lawrence, the Black Hills of Dakota and in the Rockies.

The hart's-tongue fern, another of these strangely isolated plant relics, grows only in a valley in New Brunswick, in a few spots in New York State, in Tennesee and in a corner of Mexico. This is a common plant at the base of the escarpment of the peninsula, in the fissures and clefts of the fallen limestone blocks, amid a tangle of cedar, yellow birch and mountain maple. Another fern that is so uncommon that even most fern guides don't mention it, is found only in the Bruce and in parts of northern Michigan. This is the holly fern which grows in the same environment as the hart's-tongue. The walking fern which seeds itself from one of its long leaves and in this way progresses, generation by generation, across the blocks of the talus slopes of the escarpment, also lives in this region of limestone blocks, in constantly shaded woods of white cedar, hemlock and yellow birch. One place where the walking fern can be seen is around the Bruce's Caves.

Just as strange as the Alaska orchid and the pockets of ferns of the limestone escarpment is the dwarf iris, a little two-inch-high plant that has never been known to grow from seed, but grows from the parent root. This has existed at high water mark on the west shore of the peninsula like the end of a chain to the past, one generation growing out of the stock of the other, for thousands of years, ever since the ice left the area. Some of the rarest flowers are those of a dune-cedar bog environment.

There are three parallel ridges of dunes on the west side of the Bruce Peninsula and in between these rows are low tamarack and cedar swamps. These low areas are the habitat of many rare flowers found in widely separated parts of the continent. Several are carnivorous plants. There are sundews, low growing perennials that catch insects with incurving sticky hairs on the leaves; butterworts that catch the insects on their leaves, then roll the leaves over them; pitcher plants that drown the insects. Bladderwort, a yellow flower that reaches its southern limit in Canada here, is another carnivorous flower which has a small inflated bladder with a lid that traps small invertebrate animals.

There's an odd similarity between the Bruce Peninsula and the Florida Everglades in that the drainage water flows gently across the slope of the land. The limestone of the escarpment is relatively impermeable to water—in many areas springs can be seen seeping out from between its strata—and the drainage drifts slowly westward through the soil just beneath the surface. This is cool, moving water. A sunbather lying on the hot sands of Sauble Beach can dig a hand down into the sands for eight or nine inches and strike cool, wet sand. This seepage, along with the limestone bedrock of the escarpment, creates a cool bog condition and soil that apparently duplicates the conditions of the ice-age forests.

Orchids thrive in the cool bogs of the western shore. There are fifty-eight species of orchids in Ontario and about two-thirds of these are found in this area of the Bruce. Among them are *Habenaria leucophaea,* one of the rarest orchids in North America; rattlesnake plantain, an orchid with rattlesnake markings on the leaves; ladies' tresses, a flower with tight little spirals of white flowers and a sweet almond smell; lady's slippers and the calypso orchid, a rare and dainty white and mauve flower that grows in mats of green moss or among old cedar and balsam needles. Orchids are an amazing group of flowers. One of the

Calypso

Ram's-head lady's slipper

Showy lady's slipper

Large yellow lady's slipper

Orchids from the Bruce

Small yellow lady's slipper ▶

Eugene Aliman, a former art director, now one of Canada's best-known nature photographers, has made wildflowers his speciality. He found the nine orchids on this page after months of patient search along the Bruce Peninsula. They include arethusa, the most beautiful of all Canadian orchids. They all blossom only under delicately balanced conditions of sun and shade, moisture, soil composition and temperature, and at times take up to sixteen years to flower. If you should happen upon one of these fragile plants, please leave it for others to admire.

Arethusa

Moccasin flower

Rose pogonia

Striped coral-root

Soaring over the bays of the Bruce, the ugly turkey vulture becomes one of nature's most graceful creatures.

At home on the cliffs, the "royal" peregrine falcon can dive on its prey at speeds up to 175 m.p.h.

The Massasauga rattlesnake will "buzz" if you get too close, but does not strike unless provoked.

petals has been developed into a landing platform for insects that pollinate them. Some are lit inside with bright colours to lure insects that will not enter dark places. Scents and lines of colour guide the insect into exact position. Pollen is glued to the insect's back in the precise position to be right on target to pollinate the next flower it penetrates. Some orchids produce scent only at a specific time of day to lure the particular insect they are courting. Some orchids have no chlorophyll–the vital green substance that utilizes the energy of the sun to build the chemicals of the atmosphere into plant tissue–but live off organic materials in the soil with the help of a certain fungus.

21 WILDLIFE OF THE PENINSULA

The Bruce Peninsula is the last retreat of Great Lakes wildlife south of the Precambrian Shield. Most of southern Ontario is heavily cultivated and populated, but the Bruce still offers a sanctuary. The eastern bluebird, which has now almost disappeared from southern Ontario, has retreated to this point of land, largely because this bird utilizes rail fences and fence posts of quiet back-country farms as nesting sites, and these still exist on the peninsula. Also, it is believed by naturalists, the eastern bluebird survives here because the region is relatively free from the use of lethal insecticides.

Peregrine falcons nest on the ledges of the limestone cliffs of the Bruce, and the turkey vulture now breeds along the escarpment in small caves and rotting trees on the ledges. This is one of the ugliest birds at close range, but one of the most graceful when airborne, hovering above the limestone pavements searching for carrion. Nine have been seen at one time floating in the sky above the rocks of the peninsula. The bald eagle, another bird whose existence is threatened by man's use of insecticides, nests on the shores of the Bruce in large aeries of sticks and weeds. These are usually on the cliff edges.

One observer had reported a bald eagle nesting every year in a big birch tree on Beament Island off Red Bay on the west shore. Eventually the tree rotted and fell and the eagle moved to Ghegheto Island one and a half miles north, where there were about thirty great blue herons, colonial birds, that nest in permanent flattish structures of sticks which they keep in repair. When the eagle moved on to the island, the herons moved to treeless Cavalier Island, one mile to the south, inhabited by a mixed colony of gulls. The gulls stayed, but with apparent consternation and increased vigilance over their young, as a heron will grab a young gull the way it does a fish or a frog. Another bird that has been attracted to the quiet shores of the peninsula is the Caspian tern, a big bird with a heavy blood-red bill and black cap. There is a colony of these on an island off the Georgian Bay shore, and one of the wildest sounds on the Bruce is made by these birds patrolling the coves for food at dusk.

A few years ago, a lone Kirtland's warbler appeared on the Bruce Peninsula and caused considerable excitement among ornithologists. It is estimated that there are only one thousand of them in the world. They breed in the state of Michigan and winter in the Bahamas, and will only nest in second-growth jack pine. Michigan ornithologists are so keen to keep this bird content that they occasionally light controlled fires to provide second-growth jack pine of just the height the bird likes.

The only reason why the Kirtland's warbler is not found on the Bruce, as far as naturalists can surmise, is that this colonial bird remains in Michigan by sheer tradition. But the jack pine on the Bruce grows slowly and is rather small because of the cool soil, and is ideal for the Kirtland's warbler. It appeared that one bird had finally broken with tradition and discovered this new region of ideal living conditions. It was a lone singing male, and bird enthusiasts feeling sure that a female would be in the neighbourhood, began to search for its nest. But they were unsuccessful. The bird sang for two weeks, but no female came, and there has been no sign of the Kirtland's warbler on the Bruce Peninsula since.

Thousands of warblers fly up over the Bruce in spring, island-hopping from the peninsula to the north shore of the Great Lakes where they breed, but the peninsula is not on the main migration flyways. Migrating birds are sometimes blown off-course toward the Bruce by storms. Malcolm Kirk, Resources Manager of the Sauble Valley and North Grey Conservation Authorities, made a report in the *Ontario Naturalist* about a storm that occurred on April 30, 1963. This was a frigid blast that swept in from Georgian Bay, with freezing rain and snow and sixty-mile-an-hour winds. The birds had apparently been crossing the open water of the bay, flying low as they usually do in bad weather. Their wings became iced from the spray and they were forced down into the water. The next morning the beaches of the peninsula were littered with the bodies of an estimated 132,000 birds. Within one four-hundred-yard stretch of shoreline there were 707 dead birds. Of these, 323 were white-throated sparrows, 204 slate-coloured juncos and 155 hermit thrushes. The birds making up the rest of the total were the myrtle warbler, fox sparrow, robin, chipping sparrow, cowbird and yellow-bellied sapsucker.

The animals of the Bruce Peninsula tend to be those of southern Ontario, rather than Manitoulin Island and the north shore, but some animals make the crossing of the channels and

islands. Apparently deer can swim fifteen to twenty-five miles in the fall when their coat seems more buoyant. Occasionally in a hard winter when the water freezes solid, a lone timber wolf may lope across the frigid wind-swept ice to the peninsula in a desperate search for food.

Four years ago an elk appeared out in Georgian Bay swimming towards Lion's Head. A crowd of cottagers gathered and the elk which came almost ashore swam out again. The game warden finally got the people to leave, and the elk came in to land. It lay on the pebbly beach exhausted for five minutes, then went three hundred yards farther inland, stopped for another rest, and finally disappeared. It was as if one of the extinct elks of the Great Lakes region had come back to earth, but it was probably a stray of one of the western species that had occasion-

The whole 480 miles is for experts only, but weekenders can sample the Bruce Trail in short stretches. It offers cliffs, caves, and wildlife.

123

ally been released by conservationists thirty years ago in the Great Lakes region in the hope of re-populating the area with this handsome animal.

There are many deer on the Bruce, and an abundance of snowshoe rabbits, which are the chief prey of coyotes. Two animals that have increased in recent years are the woodchuck and the beaver. There were no beavers on the peninsula in the memory of its inhabitants until fifteen years ago. Now there seems to be a beaver on every stream and pond and swamp, and their dams are backing up streams so that they flood the roads.

The biggest change in the wildlife of the Bruce has been in the fish population. Twenty-five years ago lake trout, whitefish and walleye were plentiful, also pike on the Georgian Bay side of the peninsula – whitefish and lake trout on the Huron side. The lamprey came through in the early 1940s and on both sides of the peninsula the lake trout began a steep decline in numbers. This species reached a low in 1948, but the lake trout fisheries held on a few years longer in the southern Georgian Bay part of the Bruce. The lack of streams flowing eastward made the Bruce an unfavourable location for new lamprey populations, but the lake trout population did collapse, due to the odd migrant lamprey and overfishing. Then the whitefish showed a decline. There was a sudden burst in its population in the early 1950s, probably because the smelt, which feeds on whitefish young, were killed off by disease, but the whitefish catch also fell drastically except in southern Georgian Bay.

Although the lamprey wiped out the lake trout, and certainly was a factor in the decline of the whitefish, probably a greater factor in their disappearance was overfishing. Whitefish fishermen in this area not only have an extremely efficient method of gill netting, but more important, they know exactly where to go to catch this fish, which has a very stereotyped migration patterns. The Bruce fishermen could, and more important, usually did, take 80 per cent of the available fish in one year. No form of wildlife can survive these conditions. The presence of the Cape Croker Indian Reserve on the east side of the peninsula is probably the main reason there are any whitefish left at all in the sector. Commercial fishing has been prohibited in the Indian area. It adds up to a pointed and painful commentary on the marauding habits of at least some white men.

If man's actions are not controlled on the Bruce this interesting corner of the Great Lakes will undergo the same fate as the rest of southern Ontario. A conservationist in the area recently heard a man say: "I saw a bald eagle today and I didn't have my gun." Thirty-five brush wolves were killed one winter for the bounties. The fisher, a member of the weasel family, used to inhabit the peninsula, as it did all of the southern Great Lakes region, but it disappeared with the coming of civilization. When a few pairs were released in the area in the hope of bringing back this animal, a hunter brought a dead one in to the game warden and said proudly: "I got it!"

One particularly callous type of hunter shoots any snowshoe rabbit that crosses his path – no matter what he is gunning for – and hangs the body up on a tree. The Massasauga rattlesnake, which is really a non-aggressive snake, and doesn't present a fraction of the danger cottagers go through, driving up to the Bruce Peninsula for the week-end, is generally killed whenever it is discovered. The Caspian tern which nests on a remote island, laying its eggs on unprotected rocks knowing that they are safe from raccoons, is now threatened by power boat operators who can reach it and disturb its nesting site, and sometimes trample on its eggs. One of the unfortunate things about the hunting laws is that game species are protected but there is no department of the government looking after the non-game species.

But the worst acts perpetrated on the Bruce are taking place on the western beaches. Cottagers are bulldozing some of the rarest types of dunes, ploughing up rare orchids–some of which take eighteen years to mature–and planting city type lawns on their land. Hydro poles sprout up, and to keep the poles clear of weeds the ground is sprayed, and anything that happened to survive up to this point is killed. Botanists now are keeping secret the location of rare plants in the area. Recently two women residents were offered a large payment to send some orchids to a Toronto florist. They turned him down as indignantly as if they had been offered a bribe to betray an innocent fugitive. That is what the plants and animals of the Bruce Peninsula are. They can be preserved, as can the entire natural heritage of the Great Lakes area, if it is realized now what an irreparable misfortune it would be to lose this precious legacy.

PART SIX / CONSERVATION

Man, with his increased technological power, has to increase his vigilance and carefully research the possible effects of his projects on his natural environment. The Great Lakes are a focal point of one of the most densely populated, heavily industrialized and cultivated regions in North America – or the world, for that matter. All this has meant a vast disturbance of nature. As population increases, it seems, so does the frequency with which we hear the phrase, "The greatest use for the greatest number of people." It is a favourite phrase of politicians, it sounds democratic and progressive. But a lot of undemocratic things have been done in its name. For one thing, it only has meaning when "the greatest number of people" know all the facts, and when "all the people" means our descendants who will have to take the world the way we leave it for them.

The greatest number of people will walk over sand dunes, trample the young poplars, aspens, ground juniper and grasses that hold the dunes in place, and if they do it for long the greatest number of people will no longer have any dunes to walk on, which is not what they want at all. The information that the greatest number of people receive, sometimes does not reflect the facts. Most newspapers carry a file of stories about wolves attacking people, and so many people believe them that there is always strong pressure to wipe out wolves completely. Yet Dr. Douglas H. Pimlott, now of the Department of Zoology at the University of Toronto, has made a lifetime study of wolves and has never, with one possible exception, found a case of a wolf attacking a human. The exception is the one report, which appeared in the *Journal of Mammology* in 1947, of a lone, probably rabid, wolf attacking a railway worker near Chapleau, Ontario, in 1942.

A typical report checked by Pimlott was of a farmer coming down to his barn in the morning to do his chores. A wolf, the story said, came out from behind the barn and jumped him. What actually happened was that the farmer found that his dog was fighting with a wolf. When he tried to break them up, the wolf bit him, which is something that any dog would do. Most agitators for the wiping out of wolves are hunters, who give the reason that wolves will wipe out the deer and moose they want to kill themselves. Yet wolves, deer, moose and forests are all part of one balanced system in nature.

Forests soon become overbrowsed if there are too many moose or deer; the wolf, for which they form the chief prey, tends to keep their population within healthy bounds. "The influence of periodic deep snow, wolf predation and changing forests are all intermingled," wrote Dr. Pimlott in *Canadian Audubon Magazine,* in 1961. "Under Ontario's Bounty Act wolves are killed indiscriminately, although it is known that their presence in many parts of moose range is beneficial. The payment of wolf bounties or the salary of a predator control officer in such an area is a waste of money. It is in fact, a crime cloaked under the misnomer of 'conservation' or 'wild life management.' "

One thing that is done probably more frequently than any other, for the greatest use of the greatest number of people, is the filling in of swamps for land development. This has an added appearance of progress because swamps, for some reason, are regarded by many people as substandard land – waste land at best, and at worst unsightly; inferior patches of nature that need repair. But swamps are vital reservoirs of water. They act like a sponges, soaking up water when it is most plentiful and releasing it slowly when it is needed. Forests are also vital in the control of surface water. Rain water percolates down through the forest floor, and gradually replenishes the water table beneath the surface of the land. When the swamps are filled and forests cleared and grass ploughed (as a water conserver, grass is next best to a forest) rains and the melting snow of spring have no chance to collect and percolate down to the water tables. The water runs off all at once, to reach the lakes. Many rivers in the Toronto region have headwaters inland that simply dry up in summer.

In southwestern Ontario, where most of the swamps have been drained for agriculture, all the water during the heavy spring rains flows in a rush. London sits on the Thames River where, in the spring, enough water passes the city in a couple of weeks to last it for a year. Yet in summer, the wells which have always been the city's source of water run so low that London now pipes its water in from Lake Huron. The residents are already complaining bitterly that they can no longer get a cold

In Rondeau Provincial Park, a swamp acts as a reservoir preserving a valuable supply of water – readily available during a dry period.

At Rattray Marsh, conservationists fought a losing battle against developers who bulldozed the lakeside swamp to build a subdivision.

drink of water. Their plight brings to mind predictions of some scientists that, if we do not act soon in matters of conservation, there will come a day when people in the Great Lakes area, surrounded by the biggest body of fresh water in the world, will be buying water by the gallon, like gasoline.

It seems incongruous to set aside official areas where we can go to see a natural wilderness. Yet it also seems the best, in fact, the only way to preserve part of the land in its natural state. The Federation of Ontario Naturalists, which advocates a series of natural parklands along the Niagara Escarpment, points out that the Bruce Trail, a hiking trail that now runs along the escarpment ridge, can be destroyed at any time by the actions of a few landowners. The escarpment is now being encroached on by developers, sold off in small lots and developed for quarrying. But parklands should be total sanctuaries. James Woodford, then executive director of the Federation of Ontario Naturalists, wrote in an editorial of the *Ontario Naturalist,* June 1967, "By definition, a sanctuary should be sacrosanct. The very word implies immunity, refuge, shelter – especially to fugitives. If a sanctuary doesn't provide protection, what kind of sanctuary is it? If a park doesn't provide sanctuary, what, I ask you, kind of a park is it?"

Hunting is still allowed at Point Pelee and Rondeau. Lumbering operations are still carried out in Algonquin Park. Ironically a folder reads: "Algonquin Provincial Park – is a sanctuary in an ever-changing society to man who, from time to time, requires solitude, quiet, a sense of personal achievement and the inspirational enjoyment of the natural environment – the emphasis is placed upon the interior canoe routes and hiking trails. The quality of these depends upon protection from roads. It also depends upon the people who use the interior, for this is a fragile land . . ." But the park also issues a map showing the names of companies that hold lumbering rights and the areas in which the rights apply. There is hardly any part of the map that hasn't a name stamped over it. The park is a network of logging roads. If you walk or paddle your way in from the road that runs through the southern part of the park, you will not only hear the cry of the loon, but the whine of power saws. And along with the scent of pine, you will get the smell of diesel trucks. It is a chilling reminder of the kind of thing that's been happening to the entire Great Lakes basin for more than a hundred years.

There still seem so many trees in the park that it hardly matters that we cut some of them. But by now we should have learned that there is something wrong with the philosophy, "It's always been there, and always will be." In a way this is true. It took five hundred million years and an ice age to create the Great Lakes region, and nothing man can do is going to remove it. But we can spoil it. The evidence of this is shockingly apparent in what we have done to the lakes themselves.

Scientists of the Fisheries Research Board use electricity to stun lampreys so that they may be captured for use in experiments designed to control their breeding.

23 THE SMELT TAKE OVER

At the beginning of this century there was a strict regulation of the fishing industry on the Great Lakes by the Ontario government. The size of fish that could be taken, where and when they could be caught, the amount of net used were closely controlled. Then enforcement of these regulations was relaxed. This was due partly to a great new confidence in the artificial propagation of fish in the lakes. It was believed that artificial propagation would take care of the supply, and that they could be harvested as thoroughly as, say, a crop of wheat.

Biologists are now not at all sure how well artificial propagation works, but right after the initial enthusiasm for this method of perpetuating fish populations, the First World War broke out. Questions like how many fish were going to be left in the lakes didn't seem very important. The relaxation of regulations spread rapidly so that in recent years fishing went on

Opposite: *While some species die out, defiant nature fills the gap with others. Fishermen at Long Point Bay took this full net in 1961.*

in some lakes virtually without government control. One official advisor to the Ontario government summed up the new philosophy with the pronouncement: "Let's fish the hell out of them."

Fish were caught during spawning runs because this is the time when they are easiest to catch. Undersized and sexually immature fish were taken, when leaving them in the lake a little longer would have meant not only that they would have been bigger (and more profitable), but that they would have spawned and assured new breeding stock. Fishing techniques and equipment had improved, so that far more fish could be taken in a given period of time. Cotton nets were replaced by nylon, which doesn't have to be stretched out to dry every few days to prevent rotting. A trick was rediscovered of floating nets just below the surface, so that the fish could be caught at all levels. The number of feet of net licensed was ignored.

When fishing was good, the Canadian islands around the west end of Lake Erie were laced with seventy miles of net, or enough to reach across Lake Erie and back again. This was a physical barricade that disrupted the movements of many species of fish, and they were rapidly running out of places to go. It was one of the factors for the abandoning of spawning beds, and the interbreeding outlined in Chapter 17.

As one fishery after another collapsed, the Erie fishermen themselves began to favour controls and in recent years the government has again been regulating the industry much more closely and looking for a solution to the situation. In the meantime, other things have been happening to the lake besides overfishing. For one thing, man has either deliberately or by accident brought new kinds of fish into the lakes. While other species of fish were failing in Lake Erie, one species had been having spectacular success. This was the smelt, a small slender silvery fish with a translucent greenish back, which originally occupied the sea.

In 1912, over sixteen million smelt eggs from Green Lake, Maine, had been planted at Crystal Lake on the northeast shore of Lake Michigan. In 1928, smelt were being caught in Green Bay, Wisconsin, on the opposite side of the lake. From then on, they spread at a record rate. They moved down the west coast of Lake Michigan. For some reason they spread more slowly down the east shore, but by 1936, smelt were being caught all around the lake. They reached Lake Superior, probably by way of the St. Mary's River, although they may have worked their way via inland lakes and streams across the northern peninsula of Michigan. They were caught at Tobermory in Lake Huron in 1931. By 1938 they had reached Midland at the south of Georgian Bay. On April 28, 1940, smelt were seen in a drainage ditch 13 miles west of the town of Blenheim at the west end of Lake Erie. It is still not known whether the Lake Ontario smelt came from the original Crystal Lake seeding, or from some other source, but at any rate, smelt are now one of the most abundant fish throughout the Great Lakes, where they compete for feed with other species and prey on the young of many of them and, along with yellow perch, they now make up almost the entire commercial catch in Lake Erie.

Another recent arrival that has thrived in the lakes is the alewife, which made a mysterious appearance at the north end of Lake Huron in 1933. The alewife which had occupied Lake Ontario could have come up the Welland Canal into Lake Erie; in fact, a few were caught at the east end of that lake. But at the time when they emerged at the north end of Lake Huron, none were reported in western Lake Erie, where, if it was to reach Lake Huron by going up the Detroit and St. Clair Rivers, the alewife would have had to run the gauntlet of the most intensely fished area on the lakes. It seems impossible that

THE SMELT RUN

When the ice breaks up in springtime large schools of smelt commence the spawning runs up small tributaries of the Great Lakes. For about a week fishermen go out at night to scoop them from the water with dip nets. In lakes Erie and Ontario, smelt grow eight to ten inches long and for commercial fisheries they make up a high proportion of the annual catch.

130

Mud samples raised by a "bottom grab" are analyzed by specialists of the Great Lakes Institute to detect changes in lake conditions.

this could have been done without a single one being caught. It is now believed that the alewife by-passed Lake Erie and reached Lake Huron through the Trent Canal, Lake Simcoe and the Severn River.

But the most fateful traversing of man-made canals was that of the sea lamprey. In the fall of 1921, a Lake Erie fisherman brought an eel into the Royal Ontario Museum in Toronto. It was a kind he had never seen before, and he was curious to find out what it was. It was identified as a sea lamprey. It was the first evidence of a lamprey in any of the Great Lakes, except Ontario, where it had lived in some sort of balance with the other fish since the present Great Lakes formed. The lamprey had reached Lake Erie through the Welland Canal. The canal had provided a route of sorts for almost a hundred years, but apparently conditions had not been right for the lamprey to pass through it until the canal was reconstructed between 1913 and 1918. Even after this first "eel" was caught, there were very few lampreys in Lake Erie, but when they reached Lake Huron they began to multiply, and to reduce the fish population.

The Lake Ontario lamprey was one of the aquatic creatures that found themselves isolated from the ocean, but adapted to fresh water life. In spring and early summer it migrates up streams to spawn. The young sea lampreys stay in the stream for at least five years, and perhaps as long as eleven years. When they are about seven inches long, they leave the stream for the lake, to live a parasitic life, fastening themselves to other fish by suction and rasping holes in their skin and sucking their blood and other body-fluids.

For a long time, fishermen up around Georgian Bay and Lake Huron couldn't forget the first lake trout they pulled into their boats with these creatures writhing around them. The lake trout went first. In 1936, the catch of lake trout was five and a half million pounds in Lake Huron; in 1945 it was less than half a million, and today in Lake Huron the lake trout is practically extinct. In 1944, in Lake Michigan the lake trout catch was six and a half million pounds; in 1950 it was 100,000 pounds, and the fishing industry collapsed. After five years of research a method of checking the lamprey was found – the use of electric barriers in spawning streams. But this was later abandoned in favour of the poisoning of the streams with a specially developed chemical. Using this method, the lamprey has been virtually eradicated in Lake Superior and the work is now extending to Huron and, eventually, down the entire lake chain.

Larva of mayfly

24 THE TRAGEDY OF THE MAYFLY

One of the first forms of life to hover over the cold glacial waters of the Great Lakes was the mayfly, a wispy insect with a streaming tail and transparent wings that, in one form or another, inhabits most of the globe. It has been on earth for three quarters of a billion years. It was here before grass or flowering plants. It is born from an egg the size of a speck of pepper and begins life as a little creature, with a three-pronged feather-like tail, called a nymph, which burrows into the bottom of the lake, sometimes beneath thirty feet of water, a microscopic speck in the bottom clay. In a dim green underwater world, the mayfly nymph extracts enough oxygen from the water to sustain its life, by a sensitively balanced system, whereby the oxygen diffuses into an intricate system of tubes.

The nymph lives like this for two years, growing larger in sudden spurts, by bursting from its skin. Then one evening in June or July it wriggles to the surface, where, in an unfamiliar world of sunshine, air and waves it rests on the surface-film of the water and extricates itself from its outer skin. The mayfly spreads a set of four wings and flies to the shore, where it makes a landfall on a cattail, a sprig of sea oats or the underside of a poplar leaf, and remains there during the night.

Then, some time after dawn, it moults once more, leaving its old empty self clinging to its perch. The new individual that tenanted the discarded shell remains clinging beside it. The mayfly won't eat again. It's digestive system has shrunk to vestigial remains. The mature insect is little more than a balloon of air with wings and the organs of procreation. It remains there all day, then just after sunset it joins one of the great mating swarms of other mayflies over the water. If it is a male it performs a stylistic dance, flying upward a few feet, then parachuting down in the soft summer air, until it sees an individual female darting through the swarm. It pursues her and impregnates her. The female flies out over the lake, makes a few passes over the water and deposits up to 4,000 eggs. The eggs sink slowly to the bottom, and the female mayfly dies on the water.

From as far back as man's records go, until the mid-1950s mayflies emerged from the west end of Lake Erie in swarms so dense, it seemed as though a freak summer blizzard had blown up on the lake. They obliterated fishing boats from view, and when they came in over the land, cars had to put on their headlights. They piled up on branches of trees and avalanched onto the ground in mounds that had to be cleared away by street-cleaning equipment. In September 1953, when a routine check of the lake bottom was made by two scientists – Dr. N. Wilson Britt and Dr. Thomas H. Langlois, of the Department of Zoology and Entomology of Ohio State University, who were doing fresh water research at the Franz Theodore Stone biological research laboratory on Gibraltar Island near the U.S. shore – four sample hauls of bottom clay from an area about the size of a chess board produced 465 dead nymphs, and no live ones. At another check point near the Canadian shore, which normally averaged 1,087 live nymphs per square metre, there wasn't a single one alive. The following year, the mayfly appeared to be making a comeback, but it did not last.

Today, in places where a few dredge hauls would normally have half-filled an ordinary water tumbler with mayfly nymphs packed in as densely as bean sprouts, bottom samples produce only fingernail clams, sludge worms and blood worms, inhabitants of lake beds covered with decaying organic ooze. There still are big populations of mayflies around Brockville and the Upper St. Lawrence and around Lake Nipissing, Lake Simcoe and Lake Couchiching. But there are only a few pockets of them left in Lake Erie. Suddenly the great swarms of mayflies vanished from the entire western end of Lake Erie – from around Bass Island, Kelley's Island and Point Pelee; from Wheatley and Kingsville, Ontario; and Toledo and Sandusky, Ohio, forty miles across the lake; and from a hundred miles of shoreline inbetween.

The disappearance of the Lake Erie mayfly was an indirect

Mayflies are short-lived, hence the order is called Ephemerida.

The cisco, also known as freshwater herring, thrived on a diet of mayflies in Lake Erie when they were plentiful.

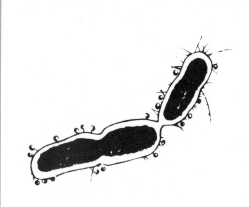

Escherichia coli *are bacteria that indicate pollution – in proportion to their presence.*

result of pollution of the Great Lakes. The shallow western end of Lake Erie has become a catch-basin for tons of fertilizer from the surrounding farmlands, salts from highways and waste from the cities. Every day, 1.6 billion gallons of waste water pour down the Detroit River alone, containing among other things 1,700,000 pounds of suspended and precipitated solids, 105,000 pounds of iron; 150,000 pounds of phosphates; over 19,000 gallons of oil, 42,000 pounds of ammonia; 2,000,000 pounds of chlorides. Waste from many shore-front homes reaches the lakes. In many communities, where the same sewers carry stormwater and municipal sewage, heavy rains carry raw, untreated sewage into the lake.

The city of Windsor is among the twenty-six Canadian communities that persist in dumping untreated sewage into the handiest streams that flow into the lakes, (the city of Welland does the same, helping to befoul Lake Ontario). The U.S. Public Health Service conducted a detailed investigation of pollution on Lake Erie and its tributaries, and in a report issued in 1965, stated that all the tributaries were polluted and that "the main body of the lake has deteriorated in quality at a rate many times greater than the normal ageing process, due to inputs of pollution resulting from the activities of man." The report contains hundreds of entries like:

"The Maumee, Sandusky, Black, Rocky and Cuyahoga rivers and their tributaries, all of which are tributary to Lake Erie in Ohio, are grossly polluted.

"Walnut Creek and Silver Creek are polluted by raw sewage.

"Under prevalent conditions of sluggish flow, the Buffalo River resembles a vast septic tank."

Many of the substances poured into the lake, such as cyanides, oils, acids, and alkalis, are directly poisonous. The bald eagle is disappearing from the Great Lakes region, and it seems likely that this is due to the residue of DDT and more deadly insecticides such as Aldrin, in the tissues of the fish, that are the eagle's principal food. But the death of the mayfly happened in a more indirect way, by a seemingly harmless, but lethal process of enrichment: that is, fertilization of aquatic plants.

The chemical substances that drain into Lake Erie from millions of homes, factories and farms, cause wild over-production of water plants. This does not mean that the water is full of seaweed. Although slimy plants will spread up from the bottom and clog fish nets, in general the lake looks much as it always has. But the tiny forms of plant life – the algae – are so dense that the pilings on a pier became as green as though they had been dipped in paint. Sometimes the wake of a boat is green. The lake is in full and prolific bloom, fertilized beyond all the bounds of nature by the wastes of civilization. When this primitive form of life dies, it sinks to the bottom, and is broken down into its components by bacteria. If it were not for bacteria, the world would be one gigantic graveyard, with all its chemical elements locked up in dead matter. Thanks to bacteria, these elements are put back to use. But in the process bacteria require oxygen. The more dead plant and animal matter there is to break down, the more bacteria are required and the more oxygen they consume. Because of this, at the time of the may-

133

University students assist scientists raise a gravity core sample from lake bottom aboard Canadian Coast Guard ship Porte Dauphine.

fly's doom the oxygen in the west end of Lake Erie, which is absorbed by the lake from the atmosphere, and is distributed by wave action, was at a critical low. Then, for a week before the dead mayfly nymphs were hauled up from the bottom of Lake Erie, there was a spell of unusually hot, still weather. No new oxygen was getting down to the lower levels. The oxygen fell far below the critical point and the mayfly nymphs were smothered to death by the million.

The apparent comeback of the nymphs the following year had two possible explanations. The nymphs that had been hatched in shallower water, where oxygen depletion was not so drastic, may have survived to drift out into deeper water and partly replace the wiped-out population. Or some eggs may have survived the catastrophe of the calm spell and hatched much later. But in either case, the damage had been done; the chemistry of Lake Erie had been too far changed for the mayfly to carry on the struggle for survival.

Nobody knows yet exactly what the effect of the mayfly's disappearance will be, or what relationship it bears to the fishing industry. The mayfly had formed a vital link in nature's food chain for this region. It produced the vital substance, protein, from microscopic plant life. It was a major food for fish. Perch, pickerel and ciscoes fattened on the winged insects and on the underwater nymphs. When the mayflies emerged, bass rocketed into the twilight in bursts of water to snap them from the evening air. Bottom-feeding fish came to the surface to join the chase. Robins gathered mayflies by the mouthful, stuffed them into the gaping mouths of their young. Swallows strafed the surface of the lake. Pheasants on the Pelee spit lived on mayflies.

More than half the adult trout-perch caught in western Lake Erie contained in their stomachs only mayfly nymphs. The cisco, which have almost disappeared from Lake Erie, fed on them. The disappearance of the mayfly was one of the factors in the changing fish species of Lake Erie, and there may be greater changes to come, not only in the fish species but in the bird life around this part of the Great Lakes. But the mayfly's disappearance has had one beneficial side-effect. It provided tangible, dramatic evidence that we have polluted the world's largest supply of fresh water to an extent critically close to the point of no return.

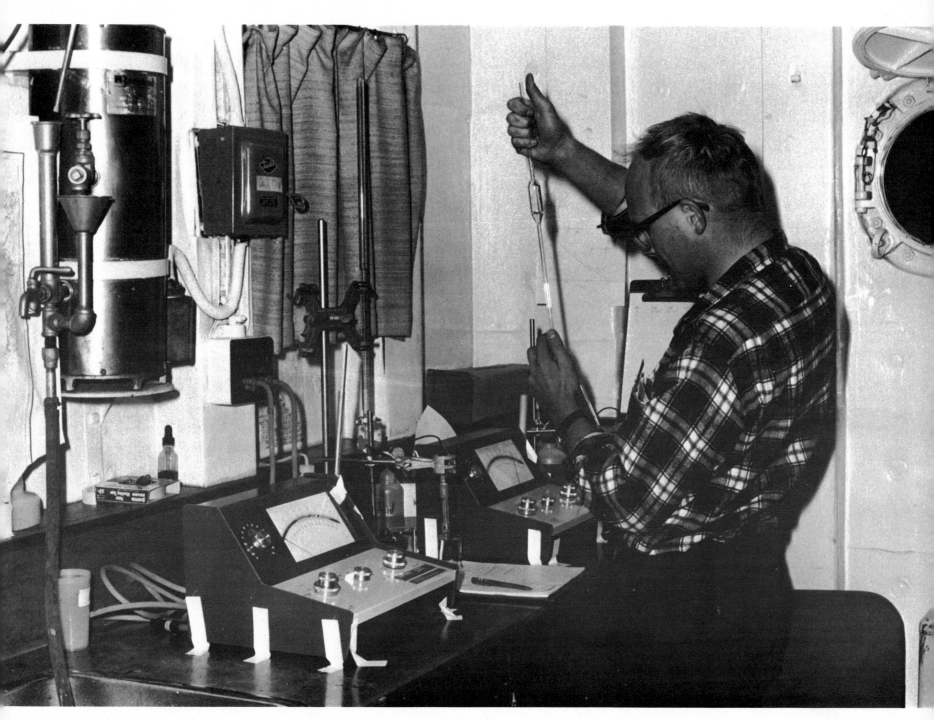

In a floating laboratory Dr. J. Kramer, of the Great Lakes Institute, tests the silica content of water to determine its life potential.

Dredges work constantly to remove the silt flushed into Toronto Bay by the Don River.

25 THE CRITICAL YEARS TO COME

Scientists have been warning us for years that we are in danger of polluting the Great Lakes beyond repair. Professor G. Langford, former director of the Great Lakes Institute, an organization headed by University of Toronto scientists which conducts a continuous study of the Great Lakes, said in April 1967: "The next ten years will be critical ones in our battle against water pollution. That's when we'll either pull ahead or be licked."

The Ontario Water Resources Commission Act states clearly that any person or municipality responsible for "the discharge or deposit of any material of any kind into or near any well, lake, river, pond, spring, stream, reservoir or other body of water or watercourse, that, in the opinion of the Commission, may impair the quality of the water" can be stopped by court action. Yet industry and municipalities continue to pollute the lakes as if the act did not exist.

Hamilton Bay, at the west end of Lake Ontario, which used to be a beautiful, quiet backwater where bass leaped amid the lily pads, is now one of the most polluted bodies of water on the continent – in fact, in the world. Water that in pioneer days was so clear that objects could be seen thirty-six feet be-low the surface, are now so polluted that a secchi disk, used to measure transparency of the water, disappears eight inches beneath the surface. The bay is bordered by steel companies and other industries that use the bay for a dumping area.

The steel companies use sulphuric acid and other corrosives to clean steel of rust and the resulting fluid called "pickling liquor" spreads a brown stain on the surface of the bay, sometimes right to the centre. The bay has become a giant settling tank for the city of Hamilton and the sludge of its industry. Iron, which reaches the bay mostly in the form of suspended particles, but also in solution, settles to the bottom of the bay at the rate of about 70 tons a day. The Ontario Water Resources Commission reported in 1964 that 220 tons of chemical substances were added to the bay every day, including chloride, cyanide, ether-soluble organic material, fluorides, iron, phenols, phosphates, sulphates and sulphides.

Toronto Harbour has become another cesspool. The Don River, which empties into Toronto Bay, carries so much suspended material into the bay that 1,500 cubic yards of silt have to be dredged out of Keating Channel every day to prevent the river from backing up. At its source north of Richmond Hill the Don is clean, but a little way south of Richmond Hill it

Opposite: The result of industrial pollution flowing into the lakes is often wholesale death for wildlife in the region.

virtually turns into an open sewer. The Don contains organic carbon, phosphorus, decomposing algae, ammonia and faecal bacteria. The pollutants come from kitchen sinks, city incinerators, garbage dumps, scrap heaps, from rock salt on our roads, from the chemical fertilizers of farms. The mouth of the Don is now so polluted that it breeds sludge worms, a form of life found in the bottom deposits of foully polluted rivers and lakes. This water can provide a comfortable environment for bacteria dangerous to man which may survive all the different treatments which the water is given before we drink it.

The most prominent factor in the pollution of the Don is raw untreated sewage from muncipal drains. This is one of the major pollutants throughout the lakes, in spite of the fact that there are no unsolved technical problems in the treatment of domestic waste. In many of our towns and cities, including Toronto, the same pipes serve both sewage and surface drainage, all of which goes to the sewage treatment plant. When the drainage water builds up after a heavy rainstorm, the treatment plant can't handle the excess volume, so it is by-passed into the lakes, combined with the untreated sewage that washes along with it. Ships also contribute raw sewage to the pollution of the lakes.

Some of man's actions are grotesquely symbolic of his attitude to the lakes. Nineteen navy ships that visited Milwaukee to celebrate the opening of the Great Lakes Seaway had no sewage collection system. The waste from the ships, carrying 8,000 marines and sailors, went right into the lakes.

Algae are clogging the lakes in many places and reducing the oxygen content to levels fatal to some forms of life – for instance, the mayfly, as was described in the previous chapter. These algae require a combination of five main chemical elements for their existence. They are carbon, hydrogen, oxygen, nitrogen and phosphorus; the main ingredients of all living tissue. Carbon, hydrogen and oxygen are available to algae in unlimited supplies from the carbon dioxide in the atmosphere and from the water itself. Nitrogen is available from the atmosphere to certain kinds of algae.

The only element that man can eliminate from the lakes is phosphorus. He can eliminate it because, except for very small quantities, he puts it there himself in the form of chemical fertilizers, sewage and household detergents. The phosphates in detergents act as softening agents that react with the components which make water hard, and therefore allow the soap powder to do a better cleaning job. It is a readily available, cheap material. But when the detergent has been used, the phosphate goes down the kitchen drain and through the city sewage system. The sewage treatment plant can't do anything with it. So it goes unaltered into the lake. When detergents began to create spectacular drifts of suds, the public had their first indication that this material was in the streams around the Great Lakes. On the Illinois River the suds were so high in places, that a wind would blow the suds up into the trees, which the residents began to call snowball trees. The detergent suds also appeared on glasses of drinking water from wells.

Soap manufacturers spent millions of dollars getting rid of this indicator of pollution but so far phosphorus, the real pollutant, which is the controlling factor of the over-production of algae in the lakes, and consequently of oxygen depletion, has not been removed from the detergents by the soap companies and is still going into the lakes. In fact, the situation became worse than ever when the soap companies took out the foaming agent. Apart from spoiling the look of our streams, it did no harm, yet it was a constant reminder of the harmful pollutant, phosphorus, which is still there.

A lot has been written in recent years about the pollution of the Great Lakes. One phrase has been a favourite of journalists: "The dying lakes," and the phrase has served its purpose. It has jolted us out of the attitude that the lakes have always been there and always will be, and that nothing we can do around the edges can do them any harm. But the phrase is a dangerous one in some respects. The lakes, including the most abused lake of all, Lake Erie, are not dead. They have been misused, and there is no question that with our enormously increasing population they are at a critical stage. But they can be saved. Over-production of plant life that is causing oxygen depletion can be stopped, and reversed, if we stop using the lakes as drainage ditches. Nearly all conservationists and scientists are agreed on this. But it is equally clear that we have to start now, not only in order to protect the world's greatest supply of fresh water – that dwindling commodity – but to preserve a region that has played a unique part in the natural history, and the human history, of Canada.

GEOLOGIC TIME SCALE

TIME	ERA	PERIOD	EPOCH	THE ASCENT OF LIFE:
	CENOZOIC	QUATERNARY	PLEISTOCENE	
		TERTIARY	PLIOCENE	
			MIOCENE	
			OLIGOCENE	
50			EOCENE	
			PALEOCENE	
100	MESOZOIC	CRETACEOUS	UPPER	
			LOWER	
150		JURASSIC	UPPER / MIDDLE / LOWER	
200		TRIASSIC	UPPER / MIDDLE / LOWER	
250	PALAEOZOIC	PERMIAN	UPPER / MIDDLE / LOWER	
300		PENNSYLVANIAN		
350		MISSISSIPPIAN		
		DEVONIAN	UPPER / MIDDLE / LOWER	
400		SILURIAN		
450		ORDOVICIAN	UPPER / MIDDLE / LOWER	
500				
550		CAMBRIAN	UPPER / MIDDLE / LOWER	

MILLIONS OF YEARS

THE ASCENT OF LIFE: 1, protozoan; 2, jellyfish; 3, crinoid; 4, cephalopod; 5, climatius; 6, shark; 7, brachiopod; 8, seed fern; 9, dimetrodon; 10, brontosaurus; 11, plesiosaur; 12, tyrannosaurus; 13, taeniolabis; 14, diatryma; 15, hyracotherium; 16, brontotherium; 17, oxydactylus; 18, pliohippus; 19, mastodon; 20, man.

SHORT LIST OF ROCKS, PLANTS AND ANIMALS

The lists on the following pages have been compiled as a basic guide for amateur naturalists intending to explore the wealth of natural history of the Great Lakes region. These selected summaries cannot possibly cover all species — there are many thousands of insects alone — but an attempt has been made to include the common life forms and the natural phenomena peculiar to this region. Readers should find it useful to study the lists touching on their sphere of interest, checking off items they have observed during field trips. Those wishing to extend their search will find an extensive Bibliography on pages 153-5; references listed there contain more detailed information on specific subjects.

ROCKS

CENOZOIC ERA

PLEISTOCENE EPOCH
Sand
Gravel
Till
Varved clay
Lacustrine clay
Lacustrine silt
Erratics

PALAEOZOIC ERA

MISSISSIPPIAN PERIOD
Shale

DEVONIAN PERIOD
Shale
Sandstone
Limestone
Carbonate concretions

SILURIAN PERIOD
Dolomite
Limestone
Shale
Sandstone
Evaporite deposits

ORDOVICIAN PERIOD
Limestone

Shale
Sandstone

CAMBRIAN PERIOD
Sandstone

PRECAMBRIAN ERA

LAKE SUPERIOR SHORELINE
Igneous rocks
Metamorphic rocks
Sedimentary rocks

LAKE HURON, NORTH SHORE
Sedimentary rocks
(slightly metamorphosed)
Quartzites
Conglomerates
Igneous rocks

GEORGIAN BAY, SHORELINE
Mainly metamorphic (gneiss)

MINERALS

The minerals listed are those most likely to be found in the regions named.

BANCROFT
Actinolite
Albite
Allanite
Almandine

Augite
Beryl
Betafite
Biotite
Calcite
Cancrinite
Corundum
Diopside
Fluorite
Graphite
Hornblende
Lepidomelane
Magnetite
Microline
Molybdenite
Muscovite
Nepheline
Orthoclase
Phlogopite
Pyrochlore
Quartz
Sodalite
Sphene
Thorite
Tourmaline group
Uraninite
Zircon

COBALT AREA
Annabergite
Arsenopyrite
Calcite

Chloanthite
Cobaltite
Erythrite
Niccolite
Silver

NIAGARA FALLS TO TORONTO
Calcite
Celestite
Dolomite
Epsomite
Fluorite
Galena
Gypsum
Marcasite
Pyrite
Quartz
Sphalerite

LAKE SUPERIOR AREA
Almandine
Bornite
Calcite
Chalcocite
Chalcopyrite
Copper
Cordierite
Fluorite
Laumontite
Siderite

FOSSILS

DEVONIAN

Anthozoa
Cystiphyllum vesiculosum
Heliophyllum halli
Favosites hamiltoniae

Echinoderma
Arthrocantha punctobrachiata

Brachiopoda
Mucrospirifer thedfordensis

Gastropoda
Platyceras dumosum

Cephalopoda
Tornoceras uniangulare

SILURIAN

Anthozoa
Halysites catenularia
Enterolasma caliculum

Echinoderma
Caryocrinus ornatus
Callocystites jewetti
Lecanocrinus macropetalus
Eucalyptocrinus coelatus

Bryozoa
Helopora fragilis

Brachiopoda
Dalmanella elegantula
Whitfieldella nitida
Atrypa reticularis
Pentamerus oblongus

Pelecypoda
Megalomus canadensis

Gastropoda
Diaphorostoma niagarense
Euomphalus valeria

Cephalopoda
Huroniella inflecta

Porifera
Lithistid sponges

Trilobita
Encrinurus ornatus

ORDOVICIAN

Pelecypoda
Byssonychia alveolata
Byssonichia radiata
Byssonichia vera
Ctenodonta myalta
Cuneamya scapha

Bryozoa
Prasopora donensis
Hallopora o'nealli
Bythopora arctipora

Brachiopoda
Lingula westonensis
Lingula progne
Leptaena rhomboidalis
Rafinesquina alternata

Gastropoda
Cyrtolites ornatus

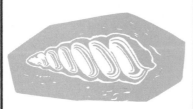

Hormotoma gracilis
Lophospira beatrice
Cyclonema bilix

Cephalopoda
Endoceras proteiforme
Actinoceras crebriseptum

Graptolitoidea
Mastigograptus gracillimus
Mastigograptus quadribrachiatus
Diplograptus foliaceus

Trilobita
Isotelus maximus
Pseudogygites canadensis
Calymene meeki

PLANTS

WATER PLANTS

HERBS

Pondweed
Potamogeton natans

Water-plantain
Alisma subcordatum

Duckweed
Lemna minor

Cow-lily
Nuphar variegatum

Small pond-lily
Nuphar microphyllum

Water-shield
Brasenia schreberi

White water-buttercup
Ranunculus trichophyllus

American brooklime
Veronica americana

Water-speedwell
Veronica anagallis-aquatica

Common bladderwort
Utricularia vulgaris

MARSH and BOG PLANTS

SEDGES

Umbrella-sedge
Cyperus diandrus

Three-square bulrush
Scirpus americanus

Cotton-grass
Eriophorum angustifolium

Sartwell's sedge
Carex sartwellii

Hop-like sedge
Carex lupulina

Beaked sedge
Carex rostrata

Baltic rush
Juncus balticus

Soft rush
Juncus effusus

GRASSES

Rattlesnake grass
Glyceria canadensis

Blue-joint
Calamagrostis canadensis

HERBS

Common cattail
Typha lalitolia

Arrow-grass
Triglochin maritima

Skunk cabbage
Symplocarpus foetidus

Pipewort
Eriocaulon septangulare

Pickerelweed
Pontederia cordata

Marsh-marigold
Caltha palustris

Pitcher-plant
Sarracenia purpurea

Marsh-cinquefoil
Potentilla palustris

Purple avens
Geum rivale

Marsh-mallow
Hibiscus palustris

Marsh St.John's wort
Hypericum virginicum

Blue marsh-violet
Viola cucullata

Golden alexanders
Zizia aurea

Water-parsnip
Sium suave

Leather-leaf
Chamaedaphne calyculata

Whorled loosestrife
Lysimachia quadrifolia

Tuffed loosestrife
Lysimachia thyrsiflora

Buckbean
Menyanthes trifoliata

Swamp-milkweed
Asclepias incarnata

Turtlehead
Chelone glabra

Marsh-speedwell
Veronica scutellata

Purple gerardia
Gerardia paupercula

Cow-wheat
Melampyrum lineare

Cardinal-flower
Lobelia cardinalis

Kalm's lobelia
Lobelia kalmii

Water-lobelia
Lobelia dortmanna

Stick-tight
Bidens cernua

TERRESTRIAL PLANTS

SEDGES

Rose-like sedge
Carex rosea

Two-stemmed sedge
Carex diandra

Two-seeded sedge
Carex disperma

Inland sedge
Carex interior

Normal sedge
Carex normalis

Rock sedge
Carex rupestris

Pennsylvania sedge
Carex pensylvanica

Peduncled sedge
Carex pedunculata

Flabby sedge
Carex flacca

Houghton's sedge
Carex houghtonii

Contracted sedge
Carex arctata

Loose-flowered sedge
Carex laxiflora

Yellow sedge
Carex flava

Typha-like sedge
Carex typhina

GRASSES

Brome-grass
Bromus ciliatus

Red fescue
Festuca rubra

Canada bluegrass
Poa compressa

Wood-reedgrass
Cinna latifolia

False melic
Schizachne purpurascens

Woodland muhlenbergia
Muhlenbergia sylvatica

Mountain-rice
Oryzopsis asperifolia

Needlegrass
Stipa spartea

Impoverished panic grass
Panicum depauperatum

Beardgrass
Andropogon gerardi

Poverty oat-grass
Danthonia spicata

Couch-grass
Agropyron repens

HERBS

Indian-turnip
Arisaema atrorubens

Devil's-bit
Chamaelirium luteum

False asphodel
Tofieldia glutinosa

White camass
Zygadenus glaucus

Bellwort
Uvularia grandiflora

Michigan lily
Lilium michiganense

Yellow adder's tongue
Erythronium americanum

White dog's-tooth-violet
Erythronium albidum

Corn-lily
Clintonia borealis

False spikenard
Smilacina racemosa

Starry false spikenard
Smilacina stellata

Three-leaved false Solomon's-seal
Smilacina trifolia

Wild lily-of-the-valley
Maianthemum canadense

Twisted-stalk
Streptopus roseus

White mandarin
Streptopus amplexifolius

Yellow mandarin
Disporum lanuginosum

Solomon's-seal
Polygonatum pubescens

Indian cucumber-root
Medeola virginiana

White trillium
Trillium grandiflorum

Wakerobin
Trillium erectum

Nodding trillium
Trillium cernuum

Painted trillium
Trillium undulatum

Colicroot
Aletris farinosa

Stargrass
Hypoxis hirsuta

Blue flag
Iris versicolor

Southern blue flag
Iris virginica

Yellow lady's slipper
Cypripedium calceolus

Small white lady's slipper
Cypripedium candidum

Showy lady's slipper
Cypripedium reginae

Wood-nettle
Laportea canadensis

Richweed
Pilea pumila

Slender nettle
Urtica gracilis

False nettle
Boehmeria cylindrica

Sweet gale
Myrica gale

Sweet-fern
Comptonia peregrina

Bastard toadflax
Comandra richardsiana

Northern comandra
Geocaulon lividum

Wild ginger
Asarum canadense

Jumpseed
Tovara virginiana

Strawberry-blite
Chenopodium capitatum

Pokeweed
Phytolacca americana

Spring-beauty
Claytonia caroliniana

Grove-sandwort
Arenaria lateriflora

Rock-sandwort
Arenaria stricta

Common chickweed
Stellaria media

Long-leaved chickweed
Stellaria longifolia

Mouse-ear chickweed
Cerastium vulgatum

Field-chickweed
Cerastium arvense

Sleepy catchfly
Silene antirrhina

Wood-buttercup
Ranunculus abortivus

Bristly crowfoot
Ranunculus pensylvanicus

Swamp-buttercup
Ranunculus septentrionalis

Early meadow-rue
Thalictrum dioicum

Tall meadow-rue
Thalictrum polygamum

Rue-anemone
Anemonella thalictroides

Round-leaved hepatica
Hepatica americana

Cut-leaved anemone
Anemone multifida

Thimbleweed
Anemone cylindrica

Canada anemone
Anemone canadensis

Wood-anemone
Anemone quinquefolia

Goldthread
Coptis groenlandica

Wild columbine
Aquilegia canadensis

Black snakeroot
Cimicifuga racemosa

White baneberry
Actaea pachypoda

May-apple
Podophyllum peltatum

Twinleaf
Jeffersonia diphylla

Blue cohosh
Caulophyllum thalictroides

Bloodroot
Sanguinaria canadensis
Dutchman's breeches
Dicentra cucullaria

Squirrel-corn
Dicentra canadensis
Pale corydalis
Corydalis sempervirens
Golden corydalis
Corydalis aurea
Cut-leaved pepper-root
Dentaria lacinirata
Douglass' cardamine
Cardamine douglassii
Cuckoo-flower
Cardamine pratense
Rock-cress
Arabis lyrata
Sicklepod
Arabis canadensis
Round-leaved sundew
Drosera rotundifolia
Ditch-stonecrop
Penthorum sedoides
Early saxifrage
Saxifraga virginiensis
Foamflower
Tiarella cordifolia
Rock-geranium
Heuchera americana
Miterwort
Mitella diphylla
Grass-of-Parnassus
Parnassia glauca
Barren strawberry
Waldsteinia fragarioides
Rough-fruited cinquefoil
Potentilla norvegica
Canada cinquefoil
Potentilla canadensis
Silverweed
Potentilla anserina
Canada avens
Geum canadense

Yellow avens
Geum aleppicum
Agrimony
Agrimonia gryposepala
Wild lupine
Lupinus perennis
Goat's-rue
Tephrosia virginiana
Milk-vetch
Astragalus canadensis
Tick-trefoil
Desmodium canadense
Wood vetch
Vicia caroliniana
American vetch
Vicia americana
Beach-pea
Lathyrus japonicus
Vetchling
Lathyrus palustris
Cream-coloured vetchling
Lathyrus ochroleucus
Common wood-sorrel
Oxalis montana
Wild geranium
Geranium maculatum
Bicknell's geranium
Geranium bicknellii
Herb-robert
Geranium robertianum
Fringed polygala
Polygala paucifolia
Flowering spurge
Euphorbia corollata
Jewelweed
Impatiens capensis
Pale touch-me-not
Impatiens pallida
Great St.John's-wort
Hypericum pyramidatum
Frostweed
Helianthemum canadense
Pinweed
Lechea intermedia
Green violet
Hybanthus concolor
Meadow violet
Viola papilionacea
LeConte violet
Viola affinis
Northern blue violet
Viola septentrionalis

Woolly blue violet
Viola sororia
Large-leaved white violet
Viola incognita
Downy yellow violet
Viola pubescens
Canada white violet
Viola canadensis
American dog-violet
Viola conspersa
Long-spurred violet
Viola rostrata
Fireweed
Epilobium angustifolium

Evening-primrose
Oenothera biennis
Enchanter's nightshade
Circaea quadrisulcata
Spikenard
Aralia racemosa
Bristly sarsaparilla
Aralai hispida
Wild sarsaparilla
Aralia nudicaulis
Dwarf ginseng
Panax trifolius
Black Snakeroot
Sanicula marilandica
Sweet cicely
Osmorhiza claytoni
Harbinger-of-spring
Erigenia bulbosa
Spotted cowbane
Cicuta maculata
(most poisonous flowering plant)
Honewort
Cryptotaenia canadensis
Yellow Pimpernel
Taenidia integerrima
Alexanders
Angelica atropurpurea
Dwarf cornel
Cornus canadensis

Pipsissewa
Chimaphila umbellata
Indian-pipe
Monotropa uniflora
Shinleaf
Pyrola elliptica
Wintergreen
Gaultheria procumbens
Low sweet blueberry
Vaccinium angustifolium
Fringed loosestrife
Lysimachia ciliata
Swamp-candles
Lysimachia terrestris
Bird's-eye-primrose
Primula mistassinica
Star-flower
Trientalis borealis

Fringed gentian
Gentiana crinita
Closed gentian
Gentiana andrewsii
Spurred gentian
Halenia deflexa
American columbo
Swertia caroliniensis
Bartonia
Bartonia virginica
Spreading dogbane
Apocynum androsaemifolium
Common milkweed
Asclepias syriaca
Butterfly-weed
Asclepias tuberosa
Low bindweed
Convolvulus spithamaeus
Moss-pink
Phlox subulata
Blue phlox
Phlox divaricata
John's-cabbage
Hydrophyllum virginianum
Canada waterleaf
Hydrophyllum canadense

Northern wild comfrey
Cynoglossum boreale

Virginia cowslip
Mertensia virginica

Blue vervain
Verbena hastata

Hoary vervain
Verbena stricta

Germander
Teucrium canadense

Mad-dog skullcap
Scutellaria lateriflora

Selfheal
Prunella vulgaris

False dragonhead
Physostegia virginiana

Woundwort
Stachys palustris

Oswego-tea
Monarda didyma

Wild bergamot
Monarda fistulosa

Basil
Satureja vulgaris

Mountain-mint
Pycnanthemum virginianum

Bugleweed
Lycopus uniflorus

Mint
Mentha arvensis

Ground-cherry
Physalis heterophylla

Figwort
Scrophularia lanceolata

Beard-tongue
Penstemon hirsutus

Monkey-flower
Mimulus ringens

Culver's-root
Veronicastrum virginicum

Common speedwell
Veronica officinalis

Yellow gerardia
Gerardia flava

Lace-leaf gerardia
Gerardia pedicularia

Scarlet painted-cup
Castilleja coccinea

Woody-betony
Pedicularis canadensis

Beech-drops
Epifagus virginiana

Butterwort
Pinguicula vulgaris

Lopseed
Phryma leptostachya

Cleavers
Galium aparine

Northern bedstraw
Galium boreale

Partridge-berry
Mitchella repens

Canada bluets
Houstonia canadensis

Bluets
Houstonia caerulea

Twinflower
Linnaea borealis

Horse-gentian
Triosteum aurantiacum

Bluebell
Campanula rotundifolia

Marsh-bellflower
Campanula aparinoides

Great lobelia
Lobelia siphilitica

Pale-spike lobelia
Lobelia spicata

Indian-tobacco
Lobelia inflata

Joe-pye-weed
Eupatorium maculatum

Sweet joe-pye-weed
Eupatorium purpureum

White snakeroot
Eupatorium rugosum

Button-snakeroot
Liatris spicata

Blazing-star
Liatris cylindracea

Blue-stem goldenrod
Solidago caesia

Zig-zig goldenrod
Solidago flexicaulis

Field-goldenrod
Solidago nemoralis

Bushy-goldenrod
Solidago graminifolia

Large-leaved aster
Aster macrophyllus

Heart-leaved aster
Aster cordifolius

New England aster
Aster novae-angliae

Small white aster
Aster lateriflorus

Tall white aster
Aster umbellatus

Robin's-plantain
Erigeron pulchellus

Philadelphia-fleabane
Erigeron philadelphicus

Daisy-fleabane
Erigeron annuus

Daisy-fleabane
Erigeron strigosus

Pearly everlasting
Anaphalis margaritacea

Cocklebur
Xanthium chinense

Cut-leaved coneflower
Rudbeckia laciniata

Black-eyed susan
Rudbeckia serotina

Rough sunflower
Helianthus divaricatus

Common yarrow
Achillea lanulosa

Wormwood
Artemisia caudata

Sweet coltsfoot
Petasites palmatus

Fireweed
Erechtites hieracifolia

Indian-plantain
Cacalia tuberosa

Golden ragwort
Senecio aureus

Swamp-thistle
Cirsium muticum

Field-thistle
Cirsium discolor

Wild lettuce
Lactuca canadensis

Blue lettuce
Lactuca biennis

Rattlesnake-root
Prenanthes racemosa

White lettuce
Prenanthes alba

Tall white lettuce
Prenanthes altissima

Canada hawkweed
Hieracium canadense

Rough hawkweed
Hieracium scabrum

SHRUBS

Wild black currant
Ribes americanum

Meadow-sweet
Spiraea alba

Steeple-bush
Spiraea tomentosa

Serviceberry
Amelanchier alnifolia

Shrubby cinquefoil
Potentilla fruticosa

Dalibarda
Dalibarda repens

Carolinian rose
Rosa carolinia

Bush clover
Lespedeza capitata

Strawberry-bush
Euonymus obovatus

New Jersey tea
Ceanothus americanus

Kalm's St.John's-wort
Hypericum kalmianum

Beach-heath
Hudsonia tomentosa

Trailing arbutus
Epigaea repens

Bush-honeysuckle
Diervilla lonecera

Trumpet-honeysuckle
Lonicera dioica

VINES

Fox-grape
Vitis labrusca

Virgin's-bower
Clematis virginiana

Purple clematis
Clematis verticillaris

Climbing fumitory
Adlumia fungosa

Groundnut
Apios americana
Wild bean
Strophostyles helvola
Hog-peanut
Amphicarpa bracteata
Bittersweet
Celastrus scandens
Hedge-bindweed
Convolvulus sepium
Bur-cucumber
Sicyos angulatus
Wild balsam-apple
Echinocystis lobata

TREES

CONIFEROUS TREES
Eastern white pine
Pinus strobus
Red pine
Pinus resinosa
Jack pine
Pinus banksiana
Tamarack
Larix laricina
White spruce
Picea glauca

Black spruce
Picea mariana

Eastern hemlock
Tsuga canadensis
Balsam fir
Abies balsamea
Eastern white cedar
Thuja occidentalis
Red Juniper
Juniperus virginiana

DECIDUOUS TREES
Trembling aspen
Populus tremuloides
Largetooth aspen
Populus grandidentata
Balsam-poplar
Populus balsamifera
Eastern cottonwood
Populus deltoides

Butternut
Juglans cinerea
Black walnut
Juglans nigra
Bitternut hickory
Carya cordiformis
Shagbark-hickory
Carya ovata
Pignut hickory
Carya glabra
Mockernut hickory
Carya tomentosa
Blue-beech
Carpinus caroliniana
Ironwood
Ostrya virginiana
Yellow birch
Betula lutea
Sweet birch
Betula lenta
White birch
Betula papyrifera
Speckled alder
Alnus rugosa
Beech
Fagus grandifolia
Chestnut
Castanea dentata
White oak
Quercus alba
Bur oak
Quercus macrocarpa
Swamp white oak
Quercus bicolor
Chestnut oak
Quercus prinus
Chinquapin-oak
Quercus muehlenbergii
Red oak
Quercus rubra
Black oak
Quercus velutina
Pin oak
Quercus palustris
White elm
Ulmus americana
Slippery elm
Ulmus rubra
Rock-elm
Ulmus thomasii
Red mulberry
Morus rubra

Cucumber-tree
Magnolia acuminata
Tulip-tree
Liriodendron tulipifera
Papaw
Asimina triloba
Sassafras
Sassafras albidum
Witch-hazel
Hamamelis virginiana
Sycamore
Platanus occidentalis
Showy mountain-ash
Sorbus decora
American Mountain-ash
Sorbus americana
Black cherry
Prunus serotina
Pin-cherry
Prunus pensylvanica
Choke-cherry
Prunus virginiana
Canada plum
Prunus nigra
Wild plum
Prunus americana
Redbud
Cercis canadensis
Honey-locust
Gleditsia triacanthos
Kentucky coffee-tree
Gymnocladus dioica
Hop-tree
Ptelea trifoliata
Staghorn-sumac
Rhus typhina
Mountain-maple
Acer spicatum
Striped maple
Acer pensylvanicum
Sugar maple
Acer saccharum
Black maple
Acer nigrum

Red maple
Acer rubrum
Silver maple
Acer saccharinum
Box-elder
Acer negundo
Basswood
Tilia americana
Black gum
Nyssa sylvatica
White ash
Fraxinus americana
Black ash
Fraxinus nigra
Blue ash
Fraxinus quadrangulata
Red ash
Fraxinus pennsylvanica

ANIMALS

INSECTS

MAYFLIES
EPHEMEROPTERA
Mayfly
Hexagenia bilineata

STONEFLIES
PLECOPTERA
Stoneflies
Peltoperla species
Stoneflies
Atoperla species

DRAGONFLIES and DAMSELSFLIES
ODONATA
Dragonflies
Aeshna species
Dragonflies
Perithemis species
Green Darner
Anax junius
Ten-spot dragonfly
Libellula pulchella
Blackwing damselfly
Calopteryx maculata
Damselflies
Lestes species

GRASSHOPPERS and RELATED SPECIES
ORTHOPTERA

Walkingstick
Diapheromera femorata

True Katydid
Pterophylla camellifolia

Mole cricket
Gryllotalpa hexadactyla

Camel cricket
Ceuthophilus species

Field cricket
Acheta assimilis

American cockroach
Periplaneta americana

American grasshopper
Schistocerca americana

Lubber grasshopper
Brachystola magna

Red-legged grasshopper
Melanoplus femurrubrum

LICE
ANOPLURA

Short-nosed cattle louse
Haematopinus eurysternus

Crab louse
Phthirus pubis

LEAFHOPPERS, APHIDS and SCALE INSECTS
HOMOPTERA

Buffalo treehopper
Ceresa bubalus

Red-banded leafhopper
Graphocephala coccinea

Lateral leafhopper
Cuerna costalis

Potato leafhopper
Empoasca fabae

Three-banded leafhopper
Erythroneura tricincta

Periodical cicada
Magicicada septendecim

Annual cicadas
Tibicen species

Spittlebugs
Philaenus species

Aphids
Aphidae

TRUE BUGS
HEMIPTERA

Harlequin bug
Murgantia histrionica

Euschistus
Euschistus species

Shield bug
Eurygaster alternanta

Green stinkbug
Acrosternum hilare

Squash bug
Anasa tristis

Small milkweed bug
Lygaeus kalmii

Ambush bug
Phymata pennsilvanica

Tarnished plant bug
Lygus lineolaris

Water-boatman
Corixa species

Backswimmers
Notonecta species

Water-striders
Gerris species

Giant water bug
Lethocerus americanus

NERVE-WINGED INSECTS
NEUROPTERA

Golden-eye lacewing
Chrysopa aculata

Brown lacewing
Hemerobius species

Dobsonfly
Corydalus cornutus

Ant lion
Myrmeleontidae

SCORPIONFLIES
MECOPTERA

Scorpionfly
Panorpa species

MOTHS and BUTTERFLIES
LEPIDOPTERA

Hairstreak
Strymon acadica

Pearl crescent
Phyciodes tharos

Tiger swallowtail
Papilio glaucus

Skipper
Hesperia leonardus

Parsnip swallowtail
Papilio ajax

American copper
Lycaena hypophlaeas

Blue
Plebeius

Banded purple
Basilarchia arthemis

Mourning cloak
Nymphalis antiopa

Monarch
Danais plexippus

Meadowbrown
Satyrodes eurydice

Meadowbrown
Minois alope

Viceroy
Basilarchia archippus

Milbert's tortoise-shell
Nymphalis milberti

Meadow fritillary
Brenthis bellona

Sulphur butterfly
Coias eurytheme

Anglewing
Polygonia interrogationis

Red admiral
Vanessa atalanta

Cecropia moth
Platysamia cecropia

Puss moth
Datana ministra

Io moth
Automeris io

Imperial moth
Eacles imperialis

Polyphemus moth
Telea polyphemus

Geometer
Ceuteronomos magnarius

Geometer
Prochoerodes transversata

Smoky moth
Ctenucha virginica

Geometer
Xanthotype sospeta

Luna moth
Actias luna

Promethea moth
Callosamia promethea

Clearwing
Sanninoidea exitiosa

Modest sphinx
Pachysphinx modesta

Clearwing sphinx moth
Hemaris diffinis

Sphinx moth
Smerinthus cerisyi

Striped sphinx
Celerio lineata

Sleepy underwing
Catocala concumbens

Miller moth
Acronycta superans

White underwing
Catocala relicta

Beautiful utetheisa
Utetheisa bella

Virginian tiger moth
Diacrisia virginica

Virgin tiger moth
Apantesis virgo

CADDISFLIES
TRICHOPTERA

Caddisfly
Linnephilus species

Caddisfly
Astenophylax species

Caddisfly
Hesperophylax species

Caddisfly
Hydropsyche species

FLIES
DIPTERA

Anopheles mosquito
Anopheles species

Aedes mosquito
Aedes species

House mosquito
Culex species

Crane flies
Tipulidae

Robber flies
Asilidae

Deer flies
Chrysops species

March flies
Bibionidae

Black horsefly
Tabanus atratus

Bluebottle fly
Calliphora species

Greenbottle fly
Phaenicia species

Syrphid flies
Syrphidae

Tachnid flies
Tachinidae

Bee fly
Bombylius major

Fruit fly
Drosophila melanogaster

BEES WASPS and ANTS
HYMENOPTERA

Pigeon horntail
Tremex columba

Ichneumon
Megarhyssa atrata

Carpenter ants
Camponotus pennsylvanicus

Cornfield ant
Lasius niger

Little black ant
Monomorium minimum

Pharaoh ants
Monomorium pharaonis

Potter wasp
Eumenes fraternus

Mason wasp
Ancistrocerus birenemaculatus

Mud dauber
Sceliphron cementarium

Velvet ant
Dasymutilla species

Cow-killer
Dasymutilla occidentalis

Solitary wasp
Ammophila aureonotata

Cicada killer
Sphecius speciosus

Paper wasp
Polister annularus

Bald-faced hornet
Vespula maculata

Yellow jacket
Vespula species

Bumble bee
Bombus species

Sweat bee
Halictus species

Leafcutter bee
Megachile species

Honey bee
Apis mellifera

Flower bee
Augochlora species

BEETLES
COLEOPTERA

Six-spotted tiger beetle
Cicindela sexguttata

Purple tiger beetle
Cicindela purpurea

Rose chafer
Macrodactylus subspinosus

Japanese beetle
Popillia japonica

Carrion beetle
Silpha americana

Black carrion beetle
Silpha ramosa

American burying beetle
Necrophorus americanus

Hairy burying beetle
Necrophorus tomentosus

Hairy rove beetle
Creophilus villosus

Caterpillar hunter
Calosoma scrutator

Fireflies
Lampyridae

Nine-spotted ladybird
Coccinella novemnotata

Convergent ladybird
Hippodamia convergens

Two-spotted ladybird
Adalia bipunctata

Fifteen-spotted ladybird
Anatis quindecimpunctata

Colorado potato beetle
Leptinotarsa decimlineata

Striped blister beetle
Epicauta vittata

Striped cucumber beetle
Acalymma vittata

Twelve-spotted cucumber beetle
Diabrotica undecimpunctata

Asparagus beetle
Crioceris asparagi

Spotted asparagus beetle
Crioceris duodecimpunctata

Whirligig beetles
Gyrinidae

Water scavenger
Hydrophilus triangularis

Diving beetles
Dytiscus species

May beetle
Phyllophaga

Green June beetle
Cotinus nitida

Dung beetle
Phanaeus vindex

Rhinoceros beetle
Xyloryctes satyrus

Ox beetle
Strategus antaneus

Horn beetle
Passalus cornutus

Stag beetle
Pseudolucanus capreolus

Darkling beetles
Eleodes species

Mealworm beetle
Tenebrio molitor

Tile-horned prionus
Trionus imbricornis

Locust borer
Megacyllena robiniae

Elder borer
Desmocerus palliatus

Pine sawyers
Monochamus species

Flat-headed borer
Buprestis rufipes

Boll weevil
Anthonomus grandis

Plum curculio
Conotrachelus nenuphar

Nut weevils
Curculio species

Billbugs
Calendra species

FISHES

Sea lamprey
Petromyzon marinus

Silver lamprey
Ichthyomyzon unicuspis

American brook lamprey
Lampetra lamottei

STURGEONS
ACIPENSERIDAE

Lake Sturgeon
Acipenser fulvescens

PADDLEFISHES
POLYODONTIDAE

Paddlefish
Polyodon spathula

Spotted gar
Lepisosteus oculatus

Longnose gar
Lepisosteus osseus

BOWFINS
AMIDAE

Bowfin
Amia calva

HERRINGS
CLUPEIDAE

Alewife
Alosa pseudoharengus

Gizzard shad
Dorosoma cepedianum

SALMONS, TROUTS, CHARS and
  WHITEFISHES
SALMONIDAE

Kokanee
Oncorhynchus nerka

Brown trout
Salmo trutta

Rainbow trout
Salmo gairdneri

Brook trout
Salvelinus fontinalis

Lake trout
Salvelinus namaycush

Lake whitefish
Coregonus clupeaformis

Round whitefish
Prosopium cylindraceum

Shallowwater cisco
Coregonus artedii

Shortnose cisco
Coregonus reighardi

Shortjaw cisco
Coregonus zenithicus

Longjaw cisco
Coregonus alpenae

Bloater
Coregonus hoyi

Deepwater cisco
Coregonus johannae

Kiyi
Coregonus kiyi

Blackfin cisco
Coregonus nigripinnis

SMELTS
OSMERIDAE

American smelt
Osmerus mordax

MOONEYES
HIODONTIDAE

Mooneye
Hiodon tergisus

Goldeye
Hiodon alosoides

MUDMINNOWS
UMBRIDAE

Central mudminnow
Umbra limi

PIKES
ESOCIDAE

Grass pickerel
Esox americanus

Northern pike
Esox lucius

Muskellunge
Esox masquinongy

SUCKERS
CATOSTOMIDAE

Quillback carpsucker
Carpiodes cyprinus

Lake chubsucker
Erimyzon sucetta

White sucker
Catostomus commersoni

Longnose sucker
Catostomus catostomus

Hog sucker
Hypentelium nigricans

Northern redhorse
Moxostoma macrolepidotum

Silver redhorse
Moxostoma anisurum

Greater redhorse
Moxostoma valenciennesi

MINNOWS
CYPRINIDAE

Lake chub
Couesius plumbeus

Goldfish
Carassius auratus

Carp
Cyprinus carpio

Creek chub
Semotilus atromaculatus

Pearl dace
Semotilus margarita

Fallfish
Semotilus corporalis

Golden shiner
Notemigonus crysoleucas

Fathead minnow
Pimephales promelas

Bluntnose minnow
Pimephales notatus

Common shiner
Notropis cornutus

Emerald shiner
Notropis atherinoides

Spottail shiner
Notropis hudsonius

Hornyhead chub
Hybopsis biguttata

River chub
Hybopsis micropogon

Bridled shiner
Notropis bifrenatus

Redfin shiner
Notropis umbratilis

Spotfin shiner
Notropis spilopterus

Blackchin shiner
Notropis heterodon

Blacknose dace
Rhinichthys atratulus

Longnose dace
Rhinichthys cataractae

Rosyface shiner
Notropis rubellus

Sand shiner
Notropis stramineus

CATFISH
ICTALURIDAE

Yellow bullhead
Ictalurus natilis

Brown bullhead
Ictalurus nebulosus

Channel catfish
Ictalurus punctatus

Stone cat
Noturus flavus

Tadpole madtom
Noturus gyrinus

FRESHWATER EELS
ANGUILLIDAE

American eel
Aguilla rostrata

KILLIFISHES
CYPRINIDONTIDAE

Banded killifish
Fundulus diaphanus

CODS
GADIDAE

Burbot
Lota lota

STICKLEBACKS
GASTEROSTEIDAE

Brook stickleback
Culaea inconstans

Threespine stickleback
Gasterosteus aculeatus

Ninespine stickleback
Pungitius pungitius

TROUT-PERCHES
PERCOPSIDAE

Trout-perch
Percopsis omiscomaycus

BASSES
SERRANIDAE

White bass
Roccus chrysops

White perch
Roccus americanus

SUNFISHES
CENTRACHIDAE

Smallmouth bass
Micropterus dolomieui

Largemouth bass
Micropterus salmoides

Rock bass
Ambloplites rupestris

Bluegill
Lepomis macrochirus

Pumpkinseed
Lepomis gibbosus

Green sunfish
Lepomis cyanellus

Black crappie
Pomoxis nigromaculatus

White crappie
Pomoxis annularis

PERCHES
PERCIDAE

Blue pike
Stizostedion vitreum glaucum

Yellow walleye
Stizostedion vitreum vitreum

Sauger
Stizostedion canadense

Yellow perch
Perca flavescens

DARTERS
(PERCH FAMILY)

Blackside darter
Percina maculata

Channel darter
Percina copelandi

Logperch
Percina caprodes

Sand darter
Ammocrypta pellucida

Johnny darter
Etheostoma nigrum

Greenside darter
Etheostoma blennioides

Rainbow darter
Etheostoma caeruleum

Iowa darter
Etheostoma exile

Fantail darter
Etheostoma flabellare

SILVERSIDES
ATHERINIDAE

Brook silverside
Labidesthes sicculus

DRUMS
SCIAENIDAE

Freshwater drum
Aplodinotus grunniens

SCULPINS
COTTIDAE

Mottled sculpin
Cottus bairdi

Slimy sculpin
Cottus cognatus

Spoonhead sculpin
Cottus ricei

Fourhorn sculpin
Myoxocephalus quadricornis

AMPHIBIANS

American toad
Bufo americanus

Tree toad
Hyla versicolor

Spring peeper
Hyla crucifer

Green frog
Rana clamitans

Leopard frog
Rana pipiens

Pickerel frog
Rana palustris

Mink frog
Rana septentrionalis

Wood frog
Rana sylvatica

Chorus frog
Pseudacris triseriata

Bullfrog
Rana catesbiana

REPTILES

POND AND LAND TURTLES
TESTUDINIDAE

Snapping turtle
Chelydra serpentina

Wood turtle
Clemmys insculpta

Blanding's turtle
Emysdoidea blandingi

Midland painted turtle
Chrysemys picta

Map turtle
Graptemys geographica

HARMLESS SNAKES
COLUBRIDAE

Northern ring-necked snake
Diadophis punctatus

Eastern hog-nosed snake
Heterodon platyrhinos

Eastern smooth green snake
Opheodrys vernalis

Northern brown snake
Storeria dekayi

Red-bellied snake
Storeria occipitomaculata

Eastern garter snake
Thamnophis sirtalis

Northern water snake
Natrix sipedon

Eastern milk snake
Lampropeltis doliata

Queen snake
Natrix septemvittata

Fox snake
Elaphe vulpina

Red bellied snake
Storeria occipitomaculata

Ribbon snake
Thamnophis sauritus

Yellow-bellied racer
Coluber constrictor

Rat snake
Elaphe obsoleta

VENOMOUS SNAKES
CROTALIDAE

Massasauga
Sistrurus catenatus

Timber rattlesnake
Crotalis horridus (found only in vicinity of Niagara Gorge)

BIRDS

Listed under habitats in the order of the Federation of Ontario Naturalists field check-list of birds (1964).

WATER, MARSH AND SHORE BIRDS

Common loon
Gavia immer

Horned grebe
Podiceps auritus

Pied-billed grebe
Podilymbus podiceps

Double-crested cormorant
Phalacrocorax auritus

Great blue heron
Ardea herodias

Green heron
Butorides virescens

Common egret
Casmerodius albus

Black-crowned night heron
Nycticorax nycticorax

Least bittern
Ixobrychus exilis

American bittern
Botaurus lentiginosus

Whistling swan
Olor columbianus

Canada goose
Branta canadensis

Mallard
Anas platyrhynchos

Black duck
Anas rubripes

Pintail
Anas acuta

Green-winged teal
Anas carolinensis

Blue-winged teal
Anas discors

American widgeon
Mareca americana

Shoveler
Spatula clypeata

Wood duck
Aix sponsa

Redhead
Aythya americana

Ring-necked duck
Aythya collaris

Canvasback
Aythya valisineria

Greater scaup
Aythya marila

Lesser scaup
Aythya affinis

Common goldeneye
Bucephala clangula

Bufflehead
Bucephala albeola

Oldsquaw
Clangula hyemalis

Hooded merganser
Lophodytes cucullatus

Common merganser
Mergus merganser

Red-breasted merganser
Mergus serrator

Virginia rail
Rallus limicola

Sora
Porzana carolina

Common gallinule
Gallinula chloropus

American coot
Fulica americana

Semipalmated plover
Charadrius semipalmatus

American golden plover
Pluvialis dominica

Black-bellied plover
Squatarola squatarola

Ruddy turnstone
Arenaria interpres

Common snipe
Capella gallinago

Spotted sandpiper
Actitis macularia

Solitary sandpiper
Tringa solitaria

Greater yellowlegs
Totanus melanoleucus
Lesser yellowlegs
Totanus flavipes
Pectoral sandpiper
Erolia melanotos
Least sandpiper
Erolia minutilla
Dunlin
Erolia alpina
Semipalmated sandpiper
Erennetes pusillus
Sanderling
Crocethia alba
Great black-backed gull
Larus marinus
Herring gull
Larus argentatus
Ring-billed gull
Larus delawarensis
Common tern
Sterna hirundo
Caspian tern
Hydroprogne caspia
Black tern
Chlidonias niger
Belted kingfisher
Megaceryle alcyon
Traill's flycatcher
Empidonax traillii
Bank swallow
Riparia riparia
Rough-winged swallow
Stelgidopteryx ruficollis
Long-billed marsh wren
Telmatodytes palustris
Short-billed marsh wren
Cistothorus platensis
Common yellowthroat
Geothlypis trichas
Red-winged blackbird
Agelaius phoeniceus
Swamp sparrow
Melospiza georgiana
BIRDS OF PREY
Turkey vulture
Cathartes aura
Goshawk
Accipiter gentilis
Sharp-shinned hawk
Accipiter striatus
Cooper's hawk
Accipiter cooperii

Red-tailed hawk
Buteo jamaicensis
Red-shouldered hawk
Buteo lineatus
Broad-winged hawk
Buteo platypterus
Bald eagle
Haliaeetus leucocephalus
Marsh hawk
Circus cyaneus

Osprey
Pandion haliaetus
Pigeon hawk
Falco columbarius
Sparrow hawk
Falco sparverius
Barn owl
Tyto alba
Screech owl
Otus asio

Great horned owl
Bubo virginianus
Snowy owl
Nyctea scandianaca
Barred owl
Strix varia
Long-eared owl
Asio otus

Short-eared owl
Asio flammeus
Saw-whet owl
Aegolius acadicus
FOREST BIRDS
Spruce grouse
Canachites canadensis
Ruffled grouse
Bonasa umbellus
American woodcock
Philohela minor
Yellow-billed cuckoo
Coccyzus americanus
Black-billed cuckoo
Coccyzus erythropthalmus
Whip-poor-will
Caprimulgus vociferus
Pileated woodpecker
Dryocopus pileatus
Yellow-bellied sapsucker
Sphyrapicus varius
Great crested flycatcher
Myiarchus crinitus
Least flycatcher
Empidonax minimus
Eastern wood pewee
Contopus virens
Olive-sided flycatcher
Nuttallornis borealis
Gray jay
Perisoreus canadensis
Common raven
Corvus corax
Common crow
Crovus brachyrhynchos

Boreal chickadee
Parus hudsonicus
White-breasted nuthatch
Sitta carolinensis
Red-breasted nuthatch
Sitta canadensis
Brown creeper
Certhia familiaris
Winter wren
Troglodytes troglodytes

Wood thrush
Hylocichla mustelina

Hermit thrush
Hylocichla guttata
Swainson's thrush
Hylocichla ustulata
Veery
Hylocichla fuscescens
Golden-crowned kinglet
Regulus satrapa
Ruby-crowned kinglet
Regulus calendula
Solitary vireo
Vireo solitarius
Red-eyed vireo
Vireo olivaceus
Black-and-white warbler
Mniotilta varia
Tennessee warbler
Vermivora peregrina
Nashville warbler
Vermivora ruficapilla
Parula warbler
Parula americana

Magnolia warbler
Dendroica magnoli

Cape May warbler
Dendroica tigrina
Black-throated blue warbler
Dendroica caerulescens
Myrtle warbler
Dendroica coronata
Black-throated green warbler
Dendroica virens

Cerulean warbler
Dendroica cerulea

Blackburnian warbler
Dendroica fusca

Bay-breasted warbler
Dendroica castenea

Pine warbler
Dendroica pinus

Ovenbird
Seiurus aurocapillus

Northern waterthrush
Seiurus noveboracensis

Connecticut warbler
Oporornis agilis

Wilson's warbler
Wilsonia pusilla

Canada warbler
Wilsonia canadensis

American redstart
Setophaga ruticilla

Scarlet tanager
Piranga olivacea

Rose-breasted grosbeak
Pheucticus ludovicianus

Pine grosbeak
Pinicola enucleator

Pine siskin
Spinus pinus

Red crossbill
Loxia curvirostra

White-winged crossbill
Loxia leucoptera

White-throated sparrow
Zonotrichia albiocollis

FIELD, SHRUB AND
FOREST-EDGE BIRDS

Bobwhite
Colinus virginianus

Ring-necked pheasant
Phasianus colchicus

Killdeer
Charadrius melodus

Upland plover
Bartramia longicauda

Horned lark
Eremophila alpestris

Carolina wren
Thryothorus ludovicianus

Brown thrasher
Toxostoma rufum

Loggerhead shrike
Lanius ludovicianus

Golden-winged warbler
Vermivora chrysoptera

Chestnut-sided warbler
Dendroica pensylvanica

Prairie warbler
Dendroica discolor

Palm warbler
Dendroica palmarum

Mourning warbler
Oporornis philadelphia

Yellow-breasted chat
Icteria virens

Bobolink
Dolichonyx oryzivorus

Eastern meadowlark
Sturnella magna

Indigo bunting
Passerina cyanea

Common redpoll
Acanthis flammea

American goldfinch
Spinus tristis

Rufous-sided towhee
Pipilo erythrophthalmus

Savannah sparrow
Passerculus sandwichensis

Grasshopper sparrow
Ammodramus savannarum

Henslow's sparrow
Passerherbulus henslowii

Vesper sparrow
Pooecetes gramieus

Tree sparrow
Spizella arborea

Clay-coloured sparrow
Spizella pallida

Field sparrow
Spizella pusilla

White-crowned sparrow
Zonotrichia leucophrys

Lincoln's sparrow
Melospiza lincolnii

Song sparrow
Melospiza melodia

Snow bunting
Plectrophenax nivalis

ORCHARD, GARDEN AND
TOWN BIRDS

Mourning dove
Zenaidura macroura

Common nighthawk
Chordeiles minor

Chimney swift
Chaetura pelagica

Ruby-throated hummingbird
Archilochus colubris

Yellow-shafted flicker
Colaptes auratus

Red-headed woodpecker
Melanerpes erythrocephalus

Hairy woodpecker
Dendrocopos villosus

Downy woodpecker
Dendrocopus pubescens

Eastern kingbird
Tyrannus tyrannus

Eastern phoebe
Sayornis phoebe

Tree swallow
Iridoprocne bicolor

Barn swallow
Hirundo rustica

Cliff swallow
Petrochelidon pyrrhonota

Purple martin
Progne subis

Blue jay
Cyanocitta cristata

Black-capped chickadee
Parus articapillus

House wren
Troglodytes aedon

Catbird
Dumetella carolinensis

American robin
Turdus migratorius

Eastern bluebird
Siala sialis

Cedar waxwing
Bombycilla cedrorum

Common starling
Sturnus vulgaris

Warbling vireo
Vireo gilvus

Yellow warbler
Dendroica petechia

House sparrow
Passer domesticus

Orchard oriole
Icterus spurius

Baltimore oriole
Icterus galbula

Common grackle
Quiscalus quiscula

Brown-headed cowbird
Molothrus ater

Cardinal
Richmondena cardinalis

Evening grosbeak
Hesperiphona vespertina

Purple finch
Carpodacus purpureus

Slate-coloured junco
Junco hyemalis

Chipping sparrow
Spizella passerina

MAMMALS

OPPOSSUMS
DIDELPHIDAE

Common opossum
Didelphis marsupialis

SHREWS
SORICIDAE

Common shrew
Sorex cinereus

Smoky shrew
Sorex fumeus

Arctic shrew
Sorex arcticus

Water shrew
Sorex palustris

Pygmy shrew
Microsorex hoyi

Big short-tailed shrew
Blarina brevicauda

Little short-tailed shrew
Cryptotis parva

MOLES
TALPIDAE

Eastern mole
Scalopus aquaticus

Hairy-tailed mole
Parascalops breweri

Star-nosed mole
Condylura cristata

BATS
VESPERTILIONIDAE

Little brown bat
Myotis lucifugus

Eastern long-eared bat
Myotis keenii

Least bat
Myotis subulatus

Silver-haired bat
Lasionycteris noctivagans

Eastern pipistrelle bat
Pipistrellus subflavus

Big brown bat
Eptesicus fuscus

Red bat
Lasiurus borealis

Hoary bat
Lasiurus cinereus

HARES
LEPORIDAE

Varying hare
Lepus americanus

European hare
Lepus europaeus

Cottontail
Sylvilagus floridanus

SQUIRRELS
SCIURIDAE

Eastern gray squirrel
Sciurus carolinensis

Eastern fox squirrel
Sciurus niger

Red squirrel
Tamiasciurus hudsonicus

Woodchuck
Marmota monax

Eastern chipmunk
Tamias striatus

Western chipmunk
Eutamias minimus

Eastern flying squirrel
Glaucomys volans

Northern flying squirrel
Glaucomys sabrinus

BEAVERS
CASTORIDAE

Beaver
Castor canadensis

MICE
CRICETIDAE

Deer mouse
Peromyscus maniculatus

White-footed mouse
Peromyscus leucopus

Southern lemming mouse
Synaptomys cooperi

Red-backed mouse
Clethrionomys gapperi

Eastern phenacomys
Phenacomys ungava

Meadow vole
Microtus pennsylvanicus

Yellow-nosed vole
Microtus chrotorrhinus

Pine mouse
Microtus pinetorum

Common muskrat
Ondatra zibethicus

Norway rat
Rattus norvegicus

House mouse
Mus musculus

Meadow jumping mouse
Zapus hudsonius

Woodlang jumping mouse
Napaeozapus insignis

PORCUPINES
ERETHIZONTIDAE

Porcupines
Erethizon dorsatum

WOLVES and FOXES
CANIDAE

Brush wolf
Canis latrans

Timber wolf
Canis lupus

Red fox
Vulpes vulpes

Grey fox
Urocyon cinereoargenteus

BEARS
URSIDAE

Black bear
Ursus americanus

RACCOONS
PROCYONIDAE

Raccoon
Procyon lotor

WEASELS. FERRETS and MINKS
MUSTELIDAE

Ermine
Mustela erminea

Long-tailed weasel
Mustela frenata

Least weasel
Mustela rixosa

Mink
Mustela vison

Marten
Martes americana

Fisher
Martes pennanti

Striped skunk
Mephitis mephitis

Otter
Lutra canadensis

CATS
FELIDAE

Canada lynx
Lynx canadensis

Bobcat
Lynx rufus

DEER
CERVIDAE

White-tailed deer
Odocoileus virginianus

Moose
Alces alces

BIBLIOGRAPHY

REGIONAL

ANDERSON, D. B. (ed.)
The Great Lakes as an Environment.
University of Toronto Press, 1968.

DEWDNEY, S. and KIDD, K. E.
Indian Rock Paintings of the Great Lakes.
University of Toronto Press, 1962.

DOWNING, E. R.
A Naturalist in the Great Lakes Region.
University of Chicago Press, 1922.

FOX, W. SHERWOOD.
The Bruce Beckons.
University of Toronto Press, 1962.

JUDD, W. W. and SPEIRS, J. M. (eds.)
A Naturalist's Guide to Ontario.
University of Toronto Press, 1965.

GEOLOGY

ATWOOD, WALLACE W.
Physiographic Provinces of North America.
Boston: Ginn, 1940.

BOLTON, T. E.
Silurian Faunas of Ontario.
Ottawa: Geological Survey of Canada, Paper
66-5, Dept. of Mines and Technical Surveys.

CHAPMAN, L. J. and PUTNAM, D. F.
The Physiography of Southern Ontario.
University of Toronto Press, 1966.

CLARK, THOMAS H. and STEARN, COLIN W.
The Geological Evolution of North America.
New York: Ronald Press, 1960.

EARDLEY, A. J.
Structural Geology of North America.
New York: Harper and Row, 1962.

ENGLISH, GEORGE and JENSEN, DAVID.
Getting Acquainted with Minerals.
Toronto: McGraw-Hill, 1958.

FENTON, CARROLL L. and FENTON, MILDRED A.
The Fossil Book.
New York: Doubleday, 1958.

FRITZ, MADELEINE A.
Story of Ancient Life.
Toronto: Pamphlet Series No. 1, Royal
Ontario Museum of Palaeontology.

Geology and Economic Minerals of Canada.
Ottawa: Geological Survey of Canada,
Dept. of Mines and Technical Surveys, 1957.

HOUGH, JACK L.
Geology of the Great Lakes.
University of Illinois Press, 1958.

KAY, M. and COLBERT, E.
Stratigraphy and Life History.
New York: J. Wiley and Sons, 1965.

LEMON, R. R. H.
Fossils in Ontario.
Royal Ontario Museum Series, University
of Toronto Press, 1965.

LIBERTY, B. A.
Geology of the Bruce Peninsula.
Ottawa: Geological Survey of Canada, Paper
65-41, Dept. of Energy, Mines and Resources.

PEARL, RICHARD M.
How to know the Rocks and Minerals.
New York: McGraw-Hill, 1955.

PINCUS, HOWARD J. (ed.)
The Great Lakes Basin.
Washington, D.C.: American Association
for the Advancement of Science, 1959.

RUSSELL, LORIS S.
The Mastodon.
Royal Ontario Museum Series, University
of Toronto Press, 1965.

SABINA, ANN P.
*Rock and Mineral Collecting in Canada:
Vol. II.* Ottawa: Queen's Printer, 1965.

TOVELL, W. M.
Niagara Falls: Story of a River.
Royal Ontario Museum Series, University
of Toronto Press, 1966.

TOVELL, W. M.
The Niagara Escarpment.
Royal Ontario Museum Series, University
of Toronto Press, 1965.

WRIGHT, H. E. and FRY, D. G. (eds.)
The Quaternary of the United States.
Princeton University Press, 1965.

PLANTS

BILLINGTON, CECIL.
Ferns of Michigan.
Bloomfield, Mich.: Cranbrook Institute of
Science, 1952.

BIRDSEYE, CLARENCE and ELEANOR G.
Growing Woodland Plants.
New York: Oxford University Press, 1951.

CASE, F. W.
Orchids of the Western Great Lakes Region.
Bloomfield, Mich.: Cranbrook Institute of
Science, 1952.

COBB, BOUGHTON.
A Field Guide to the Ferns.
Boston: Houghton Mifflin, 1963.

EIFERT, VIRGINIA S.
Native Ferns of Eastern North America.
Don Mills, Ont.: Canadian Audubon Society
and Federation of Ontario Naturalists, 1946.

FERNALD, MERRITT L.
Gray's Manual of Botany.
New York: American Book Company, 1950.

FRANKTON, CLARENCE.
Weeds of Canada.
Ottawa: Queen's Printer, 1966.

HARLOW, WILLIAM M.
Trees of the Eastern United States & Canada.
New York: Dover, 1942.

LEMMON, ROBERT S. and JOHNSON,
CHARLES C.
Wildflowers of North America.
New York: Doubleday, 1961.

MARIE-VICTORIN, FRÈRE.
Flora laurentienne.
Montreal: Les Frères des Ecoles
Chrétiennes, 1947.

MCCORMICK, JACK.
The Life of the Forest.
New York: McGraw-Hill, 1966.

MONTGOMERY, F. H.
*Native Wild Plants of Eastern Canada and
the adjacent Northeastern United States.*
Toronto: Ryerson Press, 1962.

Native Trees of Canada.
Ottawa: Queen's Printer, Bulletin 61,
Department of Northern Affairs and
National Resources, 1956.

PETERSON, ROGER TORY and MCKENNY,
MARGARET.
A Field Guide to Wildflowers.
Boston: Houghton Mifflin, 1968.

PETRIDES, GEORGE A.
A Field Guide to Trees and Shrubs.
Boston: Houghton Mifflin, 1958.

PRESCOTT, G. W.
Algae of the Western Great Lakes Area.
Bloomfield, Mich.: Cranbrook Institute of
Science, 1951.

RICKETT, HAROLD WILLIAM.
*The New Field Book of American Wild
Flowers.*
New York: Putnam's, 1963.

ROWE, J. S.
Forest Regions of Canada.
Ottawa: Queen's Printer, Bulletin 123,
Department of Northern Affairs and
National Resources, 1966.

SMITH, HELEN V.
Michigan Wildflowers.
Bloomfield, Mich.: Cranbrook Institute of
Science, 1966.

STIRRET, GEORGE M.
*Plants of the Woodland Nature Trail, Point
Pelee National Park, Ontario.*
Ottawa: Department of Northern Affairs
and National Resources, 1960.

SOPER, JAMES H. and HEIMBURGER,
MARGARET L.
100 Shrubs of Ontario.
Toronto: Department of Commerce and
Development, 1961.

TAYLOR, NORMAN.
A Guide to the Wild Flowers.
New York: Garden City Books.

TIFFANY, L. F.
Algae, The Grass of many Waters.
New York: Charles C. Thomas, 1958.

WHERRY, E. T.
Wild Flower Guide.
New York: Doubleday, 1948.

WHITE, J. H. and HOSIE, R. C.
*The Forest Trees of Ontario and the more
commonly planted foreign Trees.*
Toronto: Dept. of Lands and Forests, 1967.

ANIMALS

BORRER, DONALD J. and DeLONG, DWIGHT M.
An Introduction to the Study of Insects.
New York: Holt, Rinehart, Winston.

BOURLIERE, FRANCOIS.
The Natural History of Mammals.
New York: Alfred A. Knopf, 1964.

BURT, WILLIAM H.
Mammals of the Great Lakes Region.
University of Michigan Press, 1957.

BURT, WILLIAM H.
A Field Guide to the Mammals.
Boston: Houghton Mifflin, 1964.

CAMERON, AUSTIN W.
Canadian Mammals.
Ottawa: National Museum of Canada, 1964.

CONANT, ROGER.
A Field Guide to Reptiles and Amphibians.
Boston: Houghton Mifflin, 1958.

DORST, JEAN.
The Migration of Birds.
Boston: Houghton Mifflin, 1963.

GODFREY, W. EARL.
The Birds of Canada.
Ottawa: National Museum of Canada, 1966.

HUBBS, CARL L. and LAGLER, K. F.
Fishes of the Great Lakes Region.
Bloomfield, Mich.: Cranbrook Institute of
Science, Bulletin 26, 1958.

IMMS, A. D.
A General Textbook of Entomology.
(Revised by O. W. Richards and R. G.
Davies) London: Methuen, 1960.

JACKSON, HARTLEY H. T.
Mammals of Wisconsin.
University of Wisconsin Press, 1961.

KORTRIGHT, FRANCIS H.
Ducks, Geese and Swans of North America.
Washington: Wildlife Management Inst. 1942.

LOGIER, E. B. S.
The Snakes of Ontario.
University of Toronto Press, 1958.

LOGIER, E. B. S.
The Frogs, Toads and Salamanders of Eastern Canada.
Toronto: Clarke, Irwin, 1952.

LOGIER, E. B. S.
The Reptiles of Ontario.
University of Toronto Press, 1939.

LUTZ, FRANK E.
Field Book of Insects.
New York: Putnam's, 1934.

MACKAY, H. H.
Fishes of Ontario.
Toronto: Ontario Department of Lands and Forests, 1963.

MITCHELL, MARGARET H.
The Passenger Pigeon in Ontario.
University of Toronto Press, Royal Ontario Museum, 1935.

NIERING, W. A.
The Life of the Marsh.
New York: McGraw-Hill, 1966.

OLIVER, JAMES.
The Natural History of North American Amphibians and Reptiles.
New York: Van Nostrand, 1955.

PETERSON, RANDOLPH L.
The Mammals of Eastern Canada.
Toronto: Oxford University Press, 1966.

PETERSON, ROGER TORY.
A Field Guide to the Birds.
Boston: Houghton Mifflin, 1947.

SCOTT, W. B.
Freshwater Fishes of Eastern Canada.
University of Toronto Press, 1967.

SNYDER, L. L. and SHORTT, T. M.
Ontario Birds.
Toronto: Clarke, Irwin, 1951.

STIRRET, GEORGE M.
Spring Birds of Point Pelee National Park.
Ottawa: Department of Northern Affairs and National Resources, 1960.

TAVERNER, P. A.
Birds of Canada.
Ottawa: Queen's Printer, 1934.

TIETZ, HARRISON M.
North American Insects.
Minneapolis: Burgess.

URQUHART, F. A.
Introducing the Insect.
Toronto: Clarke, Irwin, 1949.

OFFICIAL CHECK-LISTS

DEPARTMENT OF LANDS AND FORESTS, ONTARIO:
Algonquin Provincial Park:
Trees, Shrubs and Woody Vines. 1957.
Birds. 1965.
Butterflies. 1962.
Mammals. 1957.
Ferns, Fern Allies and Herbaceous Flowering Plants.
Canoe Routes.

Rondeau Provincial Park:
Trees, Shrubs and Woody Vines.
Mammals. 1965.
Amphibians and Reptiles.
Ferns, Fern Allies and Herbaceous Flowering Plants.
Flowering Calendar. 1965.
Annotated Check-list of Birds. 1965.

DEPARTMENT OF NORTHERN AFFAIRS AND NATIONAL RESOURCES, OTTAWA:
Birds of Point Pelee National Park.

Royal Ontario Museum:
Birds of the Toronto Region. 1967.

Federation of Ontario Naturalists:
Birds of Ontario. 1967.

MISCELLANEOUS

ANDERSON, MARGARET D.
Through the Microscope.
New York: The Natural History Press, Garden City, 1965.

Conservation in South Central Ontario.
Ontario Department of Planning and Development, 1948.

DENIS, KEITH.
Canoe Trails through Quetico.
Toronto: Quetico Foundation, 1959.

FARB, PETER.
The Face of North America.
New York: Harper and Row, 1963.

KLOTS, ELSIE B.
The New Field Book of Freshwater Life
New York: Putnam's, 1966.

MCALESTER, A.
The History of Life.
New York: Prentice-Hall, 1968.

MORGAN, ANN H.
Field Book of Ponds and Streams.
New York: Putnam's, 1930.

REID, GEORGE K.
Ecology of Inland Waters and Estuaries.
New York: Reinhold, 1961.

RUTTNER, F.
Fundamentals of Limnology.
(Translated by D. G. Frey and F. E. J. Fry)
University of Toronto Press, 1963.

SANDERSON, IVAN T.
The Continent we live on.
New York: Random House, 1961.

INDEX

ACKNOWLEDGEMENTS

The author and editors wish to acknowledge with gratitude the advice and assistance of: Professor H. A. Regier, Professor F. E. J. Fry, University of Toronto, Dr. W. B. Scott, Royal Ontario Museum, John Brubacher, Fish and Wildlife Branch, Ontario Department of Lands and Forests – on the fishes of the Great Lakes; James L. Baillie, Royal Ontario Museum – on birds; Professor F. P. Ide, Professor F. A. Urquhart, University of Toronto, Rev. J. C. E. Riotte, Royal Ontario Museum, Dr. N. Wilson Britt, University of Michigan – on aspects of entomology; Professor D. H. Pimlott, University of Toronto, Dr. Randolph L. Peterson, Royal Ontario Museum – on mammals; Professor J. R. Maze, University of Toronto, F. G. Jackson, Conservation Authorities Branch, Ontario, Marshall Bartman and James Woodford, Federation of Ontario Naturalists, Croft Skelton – in the sphere of botany; Percy Saltzman, Meteorological Branch, Transport Department – on climate; Dr. J. H. McAndrews, Royal Ontario Museum – on glacial geology; Professor Czesia Sparling and Professor R. O. Brinkhurst, University of Toronto – pollution and algae; Dr. A. G. Edmund, Royal Ontario Museum – on fossils; John Levay, Algonquin Provincial Park, Dick Ussher, Rondeau Provincial Park, and Bill Wyett, Point Pelee National Park; Malcolm Kirk, Sauble Valley and Grey Conservation Authorities – wildlife in the field. Our thanks also to: Mrs. Jean Seddon, Great Lakes Institute – for pictorial references; Warrant-Officer H. S. Wilson, Vimy Barracks, Kingston – for assistance in producing panoramic photographs; Merv Marr – regional lore; Mrs. Marion Main, City Hall Branch, Toronto Public Libraries; Miss Libby Oughton, for compiling the index.

This book was produced entirely in Canada by: Mono Lino Typesetting Co. Limited / *Typesetting;* Herzig Somerville Limited / *Film Separation;* Ashton-Potter Limited / *Printing;* T. H. Best Printing Co. Limited / *Binding. Typefaces: Times New Roman and Helvetica. Paper: 65 lb. Georgian Offset Smooth.*

PICTURE CREDITS

Order of appearance in the text of pictures listed here is left to right, top to bottom.

Cover/ Dan Gibson
1/ Dr. D. Gunn
2-3/ John De Visser
4-5/ Bill Brooks
8/ John Berkinshaw
10-11/ Harold Whyte
18-19/ JB
21/ BB
36/ Douglas Wilkinson
40/ Ontario Department of Travel and Publicity
42/ ODT & P
44/ DW
45/ Metropolitan Toronto & Region Conservation Authority
46/ Toronto Telegram
49/ National Air Photo Library
51/ ODT & P; ODT & P
53/ Bill Wyett
54/ NAPL; BW
55/ BB; BW
56/ BW
57/ BW; BB; BB
58/ Peter Tasker
59/ National Film Board (Textfilms) PT; PT
60/ ODT & P; Dr. DG; W. V. Crich; PT

61/ L. Trumble; Dr. DG; Dr. DG; PT, A. G. Austin
62/ BB; BB; NFB (T); BB
63/ BB
64/ D. W. Schmidt; Dr. A. Crich; DDL & F; ODL & F; PT; Wilmott Blackhall, WB; BW; WB
68/ NFB (Stills)
69/ ODL & F; ODL & F
71/ ODL & F; ODL & F
72/ NFB (S)
75/ HW
86/ HW
92/ NFB(S)
93/ PT; BB
95/ PT; Ontario Water Resources Commission
97/ BB
99/ H. G. Cummings
101-112/ Mrs. Helen Sutton
116/ JB; ODT & P
120-121/ Eugene Aliman
123/ ODT & P
127/ ODL & F; BB
128/ ODL & F
129/ A. H. Berst
130/ ODL & F
131/ Great Lakes Institute
134/ GLI
135/ GLI
136/ GLI
137/ OWRC